The Drum:
The People's Story

Dedicated to everyone who had the great fortune to
be brought up, lived in, and visited Drumchapel.

Special thanks to all of you who helped to make this book possible; especially those who are no longer with us but made a massive contribution to Drumchapel and the people of Drumchapel. You are the reason this book was written.

The Drum: *The People's Story*

First published in the United Kingdom 2013.
Copyright © The Drum: *The People's Story*

A catalogue record of this book is available from the British Library. ISBN 978-1-907463-84-6

Cover Art © Plan4 Media
Cover Photo © Anthony Matuszczyk
Photos © Lynne Vernon, Helen Rankin

Published by SHN Publishing
www.shnpublishing.com

Contents

Introduction	7
The Comedy Factor	17
Characters	27
True Stories	51
The Transport	68
Parties	72
Oor Wee Street	82
You Taking the Biscuit?	99
Nothing Sells Better Than Hope	106
St Laurence's Pitch	112
The Swimmies	122
The Seven Hills	129
The Clubs	133
The Shows	138
Real Characters	142
The Girl in the Cardigan	152
A Week in the Life of...	165
A Year in the Life of...	172
The People's Accounts	181
The Weans' Stories	205
Time Machine	211
The Tragedies	225
The Drum's Top TV List	233
School Trips & a Burns' Tale	245
The Babysitters	258
The Playgrounds	266
Sleepwalking in Drumchapel	269
The Final Goodbye	281
The Legends	292
The Final Dedication	320

The characters and events in this book are real, taken from real-life people, from real-life experiences, and to the best of our memories. Some people, however, preferred to use alternative names, initials only, or an adaptation of their names. Their reasons are their right and we respect that. As a hint, one of those reasons is best described in this quote:

I asked the wife what she wanted at the van. She said, 'Surprise me.'
So I did.
I bought two cones, an MB bar, a packet of cheese & onion crisps, a bottle o' skoosh and 20 Benson & Hedges.
I did surprise her as I never returned. I left her and the three weans.
Her whole family were totally shocked and told the polis 'it was completely out of character' of me...as none of them even knew I smoked.

All real names described in this book have been carefully matched to the correct spelling. In some occasions names may not but they are close enough, or at least we made every effort.

Enjoy!

INTRODUCTION

They say people are shaped by their environment and where you were brought up can so often lead to being the making of you. Nowhere better describes this age-old adage than a humble surrounding and when you are born to humble origins and grow up in a humble quarter of a sprawling housing estate; you are more likely than not to be a product of that attachment.

Drumchapel, for many who had the privilege of growing up there, can testify that they could not have been the person they turned out to be had it not been for their fortunate fate to be born north side of the Clyde and tucked just under the foothills of the long-winding road to the highlands.

Footballers, paperboys and papergirls, artists, musicians, dentists, accountants, taxi drivers, cleaners, factory workers, and general labourers have all maintained they could not have achieved their dreams without what they learned on the streets of *'The Drum'*.

The Drum can boast an exotic *Druim a' Chapaill* title when you say it in Scottish Gaelic. It has a posh ring to it in the form of *Drum-schapelle* or a nice tinge by referring to it as its proper name *Drumchapel* but to the residents it will always be known affectionately as *The Drum.*

The Drum was always what we said when boarding a bus. 'Two tae The Drum, mate,' would be a familiar cry. 'Cheers mate,' thanking the driver as we would step off the bus and onto the pavements of The Drum. It always felt like home even although we still lived there or moved away and came back to visit.

You cannot leave The Drum. It follows you all through your life.

One thing most people have in common who come from Drumchapel is it never leaves you. No matter where you end up in life you will always have a great affiliation with The Drum and no matter how hard you try to work your way up the higher echelons of life you are always met by that old philosophy of: 'You can take the person out of The Drum but you can't...' ah, well, you know the rest of that saying and it is true.

If that ancient philosophy doesn't remind you to take a few steps back into reality there are plenty who are willing to cuff ye 'roon the lug if you do step out of line and think you are too big for your boots. Ears in Drumchapel have been clipped more times than a ticket on a number 20 bus – just as a wee reminder of where we came from.

The Drum was one of the many parts of Glasgow's overspill policy. The war was over for a few years but inner-city dwellings were becoming extinct. People who lived in nearby Maryhill longed for a back garden of their own and more room to live in. An influx of single-end families flocked to the newly-built estate that was designed to house over 30,000 people. That in itself tells you the scale and task of the work involved.

Quickly rows of houses were built, streets were carved out and all the necessary supplies of running water pipes and electricity all came together to make Drumchapel a fast-growing and open-spaced environment. As one resident who was one of the first to live there said: 'I recall walking the long distance from Maryhill to Drumchapel to get the keys of the house. It was the longest but best walk I ever made as it was like going on holiday.'

Drumchapel was *the* place to live. If you were lucky enough to qualify for a house it was like winning a big prize. The Drum soon had everything from good quality housing, open space for the kids and plenty of work for the locals.

The Goodyear factory *(Goodyear Tyre & Rubber Co)* and Beattie's Biscuit factory were thriving with employees from Drumchapel and nearby schemes and towns. Close by in Clydebank was Singer (sewing machines) as well as the shipyards. In all, the economy was looking good and the people from Drumchapel had a perspective. Those who lived in the inner-city never believed that day would come. The city was struggling with decaying housing so Drumchapel was a breath of fresh air – in more ways than one.

The Drum recently celebrated its 60th birthday. In 1953 the scheme was not only born but it became very much alive and gave further life to thousands of people who would go on to bring up their own children; and so generations of *Drummies* filled the vast space between the open roads and the bustling city of Glasgow.

Back in 1953 a loaf of bread would cost 10.5p, a dozen eggs 23p and a packet of cigarettes would set you back a staggering 22p.

There was no such thing as mediocrity being the benchmark with over-hyped and even more over-priced arrogant footballers. In 1953 the star player was the finest gentleman ever to have graced the game: Stanley Matthews. And a weekly wage was just under a tenner.

In the sixty years The Drum has seen many come and go. Some to pastures new to the great back-and-front-door world with the likes of nearby Erskine and farther afield places taking over the mantle of the overspill with Cumbernauld and East Kilbride opening their doors to what we now term as ex-pats fae The Drum.

Some famous people who came from The Drum have gone onto nationwide and worldwide stardom. Comedian Billy Connolly is perhaps the most-known, globally, but Hollywood actor James McAvoy is a product of Drumchapel as are the list of famous football players in Andy Gray, Danny McGrain, John MacDonald, Gregor Stevens, Alex Miller, and a host of others.

The people from Drumchapel are fiercely proud of their famous sons but those famous names have never let The Drum down and have often credited Drumchapel with much of their success.

In the later years The Drum was regularly dragged into the stereotypical hard man and tough neighbourhood image that tagged other schemes like Castlemilk and Easterhouse. Most people never looked at their surrounding in this way.

Glasgow may have had a reputation as being the no mean city but when you look at the names of the schemes it is quite difficult to believe they could produce no-go areas and some savoury characters.

New York, for example, has hard places like The Bronx and Harlem. They just sound hard. The Bronx has that throaty feel to it and Harlem just sounds like it owns.

- **Maryhill** could easily sound like a girl who sat in the middle row in your class at school. Not very threatening, is it? Well, when you compare her to The Bronx.

- **Priesthill** sounds like a mountain top for spiritual prayer and comforting well-being.

- **Nitshill** sounds as if they manufactured the bone comb and some easy-to-use scalp cream.

- **Lambhill** can almost give us a visual of an Easter card or it could qualify for a children's rhyme. It just sounds so innocent and fluffy.

- **DRUMCHAPEL** offers that spiritual well-being and fluffy comforts from the aforementioned – but with a big *BANG!* at the front of it!

Drumchapel may have been built with the bricks, blocks and cement, but it was the people who made it.
This is your story, the people's story, the story that has made us who and what we are today, no matter where we ended up in the world; we will always be *weans fae The Drum.*

There are many books written about Glasgow, Glasgow life, and Glasgow's people; and they are all great reads, but we wanted to make The Drum: The People's Story a little bit different. We didn't want the book to be based on one particular person or up one close. We are also mindful of the fact that at one time the sprawling housing estate of Drumchapel's population could have fitted into a large football stadium and inevitably we would not be able to cover everything and everyone connected to Drumchapel.

Some years ago a couple of Drumchapel residents and ex-Drumchapel dwellers gathered around a table to celebrate a festive season. The conversation revolved around their time growing up in The Drum. Many stories were swapped and the night soon turned to early morning.

The contents of their conversation was, as you can imagine, full of laughter, but also some tragedies thrown in. Drumchapel did not escape tragedy and although painful as it is to bring back some memories of those who have passed on; we felt it important to include those people in the book because after all, they often played the biggest part of our lives.

As many people and families were contacted by letters, calls and emails to give the families the respect they richly deserve to say a yes or a no to their loved ones' inclusion. Many were untraceable but of all the people we contacted and reached; they all said yes and were delighted to have their loved ones included.

The names of lost loved ones who you may see in this book whose families could not be reached have been included – not by us thinking the families would have said yes anyway – but because they played a part of our lives and brought so much to the community of Drumchapel. An exclusion would be unthinkable, such was the roles they played in the hearts and minds of the people of Drumchapel.

How The Drum was born:

In trying to keep the following information as basic as best can be, The Drum was born as a result of Glasgow's decaying living conditions from the heart of the city to the nearby flowing residential areas to the North, South, East and West.

Post-war meant a lot of tyding up was needed and the people of Glasgow deserved better. There are many fact files plastered all over the internet that can be thoroughly researched on the whole housing estate birth but in short, Drumchapel came about as part of the so-called slum clearances – or to give it its more politically correct title: urban regeneration.

Pollok, Castlemilk and Easterhouse were all built to accommodate the overspill of inner-city residents and Drumchapel, too, began to lay its foundations on sacred soil. Up went the bricks, and in came the floods of families from all over the rubble-torn slums. The schemes sprouted like concrete flowers all over the beautiful landscape we know as the beautiful green city.

Sitting at the foot of the hills that have been often described as *the gateway to the highlands,* The Drum sits like a high-chair overlooking a great plain. At night the majority of the city can be seen like a lit up postcard and on a clear day you can see far and beyond as if the horizon doesn't even budge at all.

We have to be mindful of the fact when Drumchapel was being built the whole country was not long after recovering (and still recovering) from the war. Building supplies and materials throughout Britain were not as easy to source as they would in the latter years; and the expense in building such a large project would mean some cuts were made. Many older tenants recall the electricity supplies being sparse and sometimes short. It was just part of the way Drumchapel was constructed and the timing.

There are many iconic buildings, monuments and places in Drumchapel that go back centuries. The locals know about the famous Peel Tower and the Girnin Gates. Of course, not all locals are accustomed to the ways of historical value and knowledge and as big Willie once said: 'I drank in wan and got barred fae the other.'

We always wanted this book to be about historical memories rather than historical buildings and stones. They are important, they are very important, but we have the internet for those things and it would be difficult to say something about these wonders that hasn't already been said and written on the internet.

This is also a reason we constructed The Drum book as a people's account. It is very unlikely you will find any of these stories on the internet unless they are connected to The Drum project in some way.

That's why we have Wikipedia. Anyone can grab a wealth of information about Drumchapel there so there was no point in us giving you the same information.

Of all the great iconic buildings and places Drumchapel has to offer, there seems to be less about the Linkwood flats. The high-rise buildings are part of the iconic structure of The Drum and they were built near the same time as New York's Twin Towers.

The cover of this book could easily have been of the famous Girnin Gates or the Peel Tower but we thought the high-rise of the flats would...dare we say...stick out more.

One day those flats might not be there so this is a fitting chance to remember them whilst they are still there because the Drumchapel skyline will never be the same again if and when they pull them down.

Naturally, with all things scheme-related, there are bound to be criticism. After the best years of living in The Drum we all knew changes were needed. Population growth leads to many difficulties, like anywhere, and so Drumchapel needed and deserved a makeover. It was the least the population of Drumchapel residents deserved. The tenements were no longer sustainable. The scheme had to be brought into the new century. Time had moved on and for many, probably too quickly, but the people of Drumchapel rightfully earned a refurbishment and revamp of the community and its houses.

Some streets in The Drum have changed quite considerably but nothing will ever change The Drum or how the people from Drumchapel think of The Drum and the time they spent there.

We jumped dykes, we chased rats and we swung on rusty poles. We did everything that the Health & Safety people would have nightmares about.

We made our own transport out of roller skates and old prams. If they had wheels on them they were up for The Drum's *Pimp my Ride*. Oh, and the brakes were the heels from our shoes.

We'd do anything for a packet of balloons or a plastic trumpet fae the rag man; even flog oor maw's fur coats.

We stayed out as late as we could and played games in the dark. The only way we could be detected was by our unique excited screams. We enjoyed great days in the fields playing Cowboys & Indians where the Indians were allowed to win.

We'd climb trees that high you needed help to get back down again and we scaled roofs of schools and properties just so we could prove we could do it.

We ate and drank anything that was put down to us. We even shared one bottle of *skoosh* between a crowd; only wiping the bottle's rim with the sleeve to wipe away the leftover saliva. Pre-potential floaters we'd probably call them these days.

If a teacher belted us we'd expect the same again from our parents: because the teacher *must* have been right.

Adults commanded authority and were respected – and rightly so.

I will not change my accent
just because of where I am
I have this accent because of who I am
and who I am
is a result of where I'm from
and where I'm from
has made me who I am....

The Drum:
The Comedy Factor

Drumchapel has always been a funny place to live. There is just something about Glasgow on a whole that has opened up the box to pop out comedic geniuses and not all of them have gone on to make a living from it. They don't have to; they make people laugh and laughter can oftentimes make a difference.

Glasgow, as all of us Glaswegians know, seems to have this blend of mix races and cultures that has come together in one big pot and it has stewed up a fine serving roast of belly-tickling patter.

The Irish brought with them their humour as did the Italians and the Jewish people who came to Glasgow to settle. The Polish community have been known to bring their stern and rigid dry style, too. It is a great mixture and in the rubbles of life's hardship you will always find the best against-all-odds material.

This magical mix has been to Glasgow's great advantage and the city has often been referred to as the funniest city in the world.

Now, New Yorkers might have something to say about that and the very finest of them all, George Carlin, was a New Yorker, but he was born from Irish heritage.

If Carlin's family had travelled the short journey East to Glasgow instead of out West to New York there is no doubt George Carlin would still be regarded as one of the world's greatest-ever comedians…arguably, of course.

Billy Connolly has had the honour of that vote in a poll of 100 Top Comedians. Had his family sailed West to New York, there is every chance the Big Yin would have made it there, too. If you can make it from Irish and Scots origins you can make it anywhere. Now there must be a song in there, surely?

Meanwhile back at The Drum…

We've had a fair share of really funny people and for so long most of us have had that feeling someone from The Drum will step up and take hold of the comedy scene by its short and circuits. Rob Kane, a Drumchapel boy, looks to be a possible candidate to go all the way. He might not reach Connolly status but neither will anyone as it is quite unthinkable for any new artist to have the staying power of being at the top for a handful of decades. It is not shedding any negative light on any hopeful but the world is much different now; it moves a lot quicker and even the very best of anyone at anything these days will find it quite a task to have the same amount of time at the top as the predecessors.

Rob Kane is young, has time on his side, and can only grow but he is a fine and upstanding comedian with a future that is in his own hands. It is up to him but his Drumchapel background will already have told him that.

In Drumchapel we've seen so many funny people who may not have gone onto enjoy a life in the comedy world but the ones who have can lay some claim their way. Most comedians will tell you they get their inspiration and material from their surroundings. Kevin Bridges, who grew up quite near The Drum but just not close enough to be featured more in this book, seems to work with his surroundings and the people around him.

Hugh Cairns, not a Drumchapel boy, but knew where Billy Connolly drew his inspiration from. Hugh said: 'Connolly was funny at a young age but there were even funnier guys than him. Bill's material seemed to be centred around those funny people, the place, and the behaviour. Connolly would talk about places and people from Springburn to Drumchapel and I knew who he was talking about.'

The collection of material that follows comes from The Drum. The jokes, the characters, the material and commentary. They all come from Drumchapel. Granted, some stories may have been passed down and could have happened to anyone, anywhere, in a place like The Drum, but they are all Drum-related, happened in The Drum, and to someone from The Drum.

The Funnies: *Lollipop sticks and bubble gum jokes fae the van…aye right! They were much better.*

A collection of true stories and jokes that were created in The Drum:

I first learned there was no such thing as Santa Claus when I lived in Drumchapel. I blame that wee bugger up the stairs from me for letting the cat out the bag. I should have known better – he was two years older than me.

Anyway, I was completely shattered and I wanted

the world to end. I locked myself in my room for days on end and I never ate for about a week.

It got so bad my poor maw had to hand in my sick line to my boss.

****

A Rolls Royce stopped in to fuel up in the petrol station on the Boulevard. It would be the last stop on the way to the highlands. Apparently the same car had tanked up at this very station before. There are not many Rolls Royce cars in The Drum so it was an attraction.

What was even more of a head-turner was who was in the car.

There were some people in the forecourt who were screaming, 'It's him! It's him!' but not everyone got caught up in the hysteria.

The guy in the car was signing autographs for the screaming autograph hunters when a wee boy approached the vehicle to get his. Everybody was scrambling about for a pen and paper.

As the Rolls Royce drove away the wee boy looked at the signature and asked an adult near him if she could read out the name.

'That wiz Paul McCartney,' she said, excitedly, as she looked at the boy's note.

The boy crumpled the piece of paper up and threw it away and moaned, 'That's pish, Ah thought it wiz Ian Redford.'

*Ian Redford played for Rangers FC at the time and he bore a resemblance to the Beatle, Paul McCartney. Redford was once in the newspaper with his photo beside

McCartney's in a look-alike article.

****

Two wee boys were approached by an American man and wife who had come to Scotland for a holiday. The boys had never seen anything like them in real-life. The only Americans they'd seen were the ones on TV and their accents were just magnificent.

They were heading North and the boys were playing football near the Boulevard. The man was very large and broad but his fingers were fat. The boys were fascinated as they'd never seen anyone with fat fingers before. They looked rich.

The fascination for the American couple was about to be reciprocated because the man asked the wee boys to say something in 'Scotch'.

He and his wife could not get over the Scottish accent. 'They were more fascinated by us than we were of them,' said one of the boys, now an adult.

The reason why they stopped had something to do with the luggage they had on their roof-rack. I have to stress they did not approach the boys. The boys approached the couple as they thought they might need some help.

They were extremely friendly.

'Say something in Scotch. My wife can't get over your accents.'

'Whit d'ye want us tae say?'

'That's it, just that what you said. Here, now go buy yourselves some ice-cream.'

The man handed over a crispy five pound note and waved the boys off.

As the car drove off the two wee boys stood at the

side of the Boulevard staring into this fiver.

'You gonnae tell yer maw?' said one of the boys.

'Naw, ur you?'

'Pffft, nae chance.'

'Whit kin ye buy for a fiver?'

'Ah don't know but whatever it is it's gonnae be hunners o' it.'

'He jist gave us a fiver for talking Scottish.'

'Ah know, d'ye want tae wait here tae see if mare Americans turn up?'

A fiver in 1973 was a lot of money. It got the two wee boys a lot of sweeties. God bless the USA.

****

The value of the fiver was soon to be increased when some months later another two wee boys were playing in the long grass across from their house. They stumbled upon a brown bag with the contents containing a half bottle of whisky and a scrunched up five pound note. It was sent from heaven. They could not hold their excitement. One of the boys said he had to tell his dad and so both went to the father. He was as impressed as the boys were and warned them not to say a word.

Quickly the boy's father grabbed the bag and said, 'Here, ye kin keep the money, Ah'm takin' this bloody whisky.'

****

A young girl was proud and pleased with her way of talking. She was polite and knew all the right words and how to pronounce them properly. She would often give stick to the other children if they did not adhere to the rules of proper English.

She was a school teacher in the making.

An incident arose whereby the police were called and they asked some kids some questions.

'And what way did you come?' asked the policeman.

'Up through Kendoon,' replied a young girl.

The wee polite girl interrupted the flow of conversation and instructed both the police officer and the other kid, 'It's not Kendoon, it's Kendown.'

****

As he looked inside the dark cupboard for a jacket to wear to go to the pub his 4-year-old daughter said, 'Dad, don't wear that navy blue one.'

'Why is that, hen? asked the father.

'Because when you wear that blue jacket you always trip up the stairs, smash something and waken everybody up.'

'*D-aaaad!* Kin Ah get a biscuit?' shouted the wee boy from his bedroom.

'Naw, yer no gettin' wan, noo get tae sleep.'

'Ah'm hungry.'

'Good, you'll enjoy yer breakfast better in the mornin'.'

****

Mary: 'Willie, Ah've got a wee puzzle here. 4 up and 2 across.'

Willie: 'Ah bet ye it's her wi the five weans up in number 74?'

****

Big Davey's road rage:

'Ah hud tae gie the bastart the middle finger. He wiz gettin' in the way of an argument between me and a Chrysler Sunbeam.'

****

Naw, life disnae begin at 40. If ye don't believe me then wait until yer forty-five then try strippin' a Cindy Doll right doon tae the buff.

Then throw yer parachute action man oot a close windae and see how long it takes for both the polis comin' tae charge ye wi a sexual offence and the Anti-terror squad accusing ye of havin' taken part in training in Pakistan tae learn how tae make the wee man's eyes move.

****

My ex-wife should be captain of a tug-of-war team because she really has trouble letting go.

****

'I would never go to China, no fucking way, man.
It has nothing to do with their atrocious human

rights. It has fuck all to do with the way they treat household pets and it has nothing remotely to do with me being really politically against their government regime.

It is just that I am terrified that their food might not taste the same as it does in Drumry Road.'

****

I do recall in my childhood a certain Basil Brush.

Or in today's politically challenged world he would probably be referred to as:

A cunningly carnivorous mammal with an attached cleansing assistant.

****

Due to the whole Political Correctness thing going on right now, Punch & Judy have had to change their names and stage set.

Punch has been replaced by A Fake Non Contact Sparring Blow

And Judy has been replaced by a group of Partner Equality Enthusiasts.

****

They will no longer be able to swap leather on stage; instead they will be required to take part in a new-age, political correctness reality show titled: Strictly Come Punching.

****

Even the simple noun of 'Snowman' will be no longer acceptable with these equality arseholes.

By next winter it will most likely be deemed sexist to say you built a snowman unless you say the little fat bastard in your garden was formed in a sculptured-like bodily pattern made directly from frozen water molecules that excludes any genitalia.

****

I remember visiting one of my old neighbours, as I had always done each Sunday. I became a vegetarian but never really explained to my old neighbours as they were quite old and from the old school of life. They just wouldn't understand. How could I possibly tell them I have a rule that I do not eat anything that moves, has a face, or has a mum & dad?

Anyway, she wanted me to stay for dinner. This is how the conversation went…

'Are ye stayin' fir yer tea, son? We've a lovely steak pie in the oven.'

'No thanks. I don't eat meat anymore.'

'Whit d'ye mean, ye don't eat meat anymare?'

'Well, I am a vegetarian and vegetarians don't eat meat.'

'How no? Is that some kinda religion, or somethin'?'

'No, nothing like that. I just feel it wrong to eat animals.'

'Well, d'ye jist want a wee piece and sausage then, son?'

The Drum:
Characters

The Drum is teeming with characters that have made us laugh for decades. Everybody has a daft uncle, an unconscious comedian, *(supposed to be sub conscious but some of the patter would knock you out)* and a funny true tale to tell.

The following characters may have their names as they are/were but some have been changed to protect the guilty.

Character:
Archie

Big Archie was only average height but his presence was huge. He was so often referred to as *big Archie fae up the sterrs.* In fact, so much so the weans in the street thought it was his second name.

He was a rather larger-than-life character who made us laugh and think at the same time. A bright, humble and unassuming man.

Enjoy Archie's Antics…

Archie's Introduction:

Archie *fae up the sterrs* has been retired for eighteen years from the shipyards but he still gets up at 6am to make his pieces.

Archie's daughter wasn't aware her dad had a drink problem – until she saw him sober one night.

She said: 'The off-sales was shut and it was the first time in years my dad couldn't get a drink. On this day his glaeckit expression had been replaced by a straight-laced, coherent, and understanding coupon. It was then it hit me: that's my da!'

Archie's daughter wanted to get married in Gretna Green. He said: 'Nae chance, she's getting' merrit in silky white, like every other lassie.'

Archie fae up the sterrs on Dougie & Tam:

'They two are always uptae something. Last week big Tam and his missus got nabbed makin' love oan an overnight sleeper train. Tam's wife was raging when she got caught. She wiz black affronted, pure totally embarrassed, the young lassie wiz…as she said she never even hud a ticket.

Archie and the taxman:

When Archie fae up the sterrs was self-employed he had a visit from the taxman at his house. As he opened the door to a very loud and authoritarian knock, the taxman asked, 'Mr Archibald *(second name withheld)*. I am from the Inland Revenue and I am up here looking for the sum of £6000.' To which Archie fae up the sterrs replied, 'Is that right, son? Haud oan tae a get ma jaecket and I'll come oot and gie ye a haun.'

Archie fae up the sterrs on Political Correctness:

It's aw gaun mad! The Average White Band will soon

need tae change their name tae: A Normal Shade Band or The Band With The Equal Colour. Duran Duran must surely imply we all have a stutter then, eh? Is that no a wee bit cheeky tae those wi a speech problem?

Archie fae up the sterrs on the polis:

I love films and I love tae wait until the credits come up so that Ah can see when the film wiz made. They always use Roman numerals tae tell ye the year. I picked up on this and started tae use it tae ma advantage. Anytime wan o' they young polisman try tae huckle me when I'm bevvied and ask me details a usually gie them it like this...

Polisman: 'Name, Sir?'
Me: 'Archie.'
Polisman: 'Age?'
Me: 'LXVIII.'
Polisman: 'Date of birth?'
Me: 'MCMXL.'
Polisman: 'Address?'
Me: 'CXLVIII Great Western Road, Sir.'

Efter a while they jist let me go. I don't think they can be bothered wi the paperwork. It works every time.

Archie's take on the modern world:

The west of Scotland has had a boom of babies born by caesarean section in the last couple of decades. You can see full evidence of this report in any given retail car park on a Saturday afternoon. They all get oot of their cars through the sunroof.

Archie on Christmas:

When someone gives me a terribly unwanted Christmas present I don't throw it out; I keep it for the next year. I re-wrap them and hand them out to people. Well, it saves money and as I am a pensioner I cannot afford to go down the road of splashing the cash I don't have. The downside is: I have so many unwanted gifts from so many people I usually end up giving the same present back to the same people who gave me the terribly unwanted gift in the first place.

Archie on his ex-wife:

The definition of mixed emotions is watching my ex-wife driving over a busy railway crossing warning signal in my brand new 4x4 jeep that the courts awarded her.

Archie on the news:

Archie read an article with a rather frightening statistic in the papers that read...

A man in Glasgow is knocked down in the city centre every three weeks.

Archie was asked about his thoughts on this statistic. He said, 'Daft bugger, ye'd think he'd learn tae use the green man.'

Archie's ex-wife's diet:

Archie's wife *(they've been divorced for a while now)* was once recommended to go on a sauerkraut diet. It was great but the side effects were a lot of wind.

One day Archie and his then wife were out shopping. They parked the car and headed into the Main Street shops.

Once inside a shop she felt wind coming on and immediately fled to the car. She ran and ran, opened the passenger door, sat down and let rip. It was a cracker, the loudest yet.

Just as she belched; relieving her bloated stomach, she turned round and there was a guy in the driver's seat. She had gone to the wrong car!

In a flash she opened the door and bolted as fast as she could; her face bright red with obvious embarrassment.

As she ran down the Main Street Archie beeped the horn and drove alongside her. She jumped in and yelled, 'Quick, let's get out of here. You'll never believe what just happened there.'

A few seconds later she looked in the mirror and saw the driver following her and Archie.

'Quick, Archie, get the foot down, that guy is following us.'

Archie was a bit confused and asked, 'What the hell did you do to make the guy follow us?'

Archie then tried to lose the guy but he kept following Archie and his wife.

At the lights they had no option but to stop at red.

A flush came over Archie's wife as the guy got out of his car at the lights and approached Archie's passenger window.

Archie's wife, slowly and with fear, rolled the window down.

The guy said, 'Alright missus? Ye furgoat yer handbag!'

Archie with the papers:

Archie was reading the newspaper when he came across this article…

MAN WANTED FOR ARMED ROBBERY AND SERIOUS ASSAULT IN CITY CENTRE

Archie told his close friends he was thinking about applying.

Archie on his failed life:

I guess I am a bit like a travelling salesman, except that I don't actually have anything for sale, but I still live in hope that someone will eventually be stupit enough tae make a purchase.

Archie on the news:

A woman claims depression caused her weight to balloon to at least four times her normal size. Naw it wisnae – it was her EATING that caused her weight to balloon to four times her normal size. You don't go to your bed one night pissed off because your relationship sucks, you have no money, and lots of debt, and you feel terrible; then wake up the next day and you find you can't fit through doorways any more. I don't know but maybe, just maybe, it was something to do with the cakes, crisps, and bottles of ginger she scoffed that caused her weight increase.

Archie's Library:

Archie fae up the sterrs bought a nice bookshelf and went to a bargain bookstore and filled his shelves up with books on a variety of subjects like: law, medicine, history and philosophy.

His neighbours were well impressed, prompting many to ask, 'Are ye studying fur somethin', Archie?'

To which Archie replied, 'Naw, ur ye kiddin'? Ah cannae read things like that. It's just a display so that when burglars come in through the night they will shine their torches at each other as they rumble through ma drawers fur dosh and wan o' them will say, 'Haw Rab, look at this! This guy's a right clever bastard!'

Archie on getting older:

In your late teens somebody can ask ye if ye want a pint and ye don't care whit kind a pint it is, ye jist swally it.

In your early twenties ye start tae experiment wi different types of beers, and in yer late twenties ye've found yer ideal swally. It might be a heavy or a lager but ye've sorted it oot by then.

Then in yer thirties ye start tae experiment wi spirits then in yer forties ye analyze a pint, not by a lager or a heavy, but by the calorie intake.

Then in yer fifties ye find the only wan that does the trick is the whisky and that's aw yer left wi.

Character:
Big Auntie Madge

Big Auntie Madge is a self-proclaimed psychologist who has spent decades helping her neighbours with their every day problems.

She now has her own column in the popular Dafty News and is regarded as the best agony aunt in the business.

She said: 'Ah don't help people get aff the drink, Ah help people cope wi staying oan it.'

Her slogan outside her office up the close reads:

**Nae matter whit yer problem is, Ah can help ye.
The drink, the drugs – disnae matter –
Ah kin sell ye both.**

Big Auntie Madge is also known for her philosophy, with her signature line:

**'The only things guaranteed in life are: death,
taxes, and that iron boards will always make a
squeaky noise.'**

Madge is one of The Drum's toughest characters. She spent a part of her life looking after people's problems after living through most of them herself. The straight-talking lady grew up on the Clydeside before becoming one of the scheme's earliest overspill weans.

She has often described The Drum as 'playing the biggest part of her life.'

'I came from a crowded tenement near the docks. It was a tough upbringing but a very close and loving one. I think this is where I got my empathy from as we were always looking out for each other. When I moved to Drumchapel it was a wide-eye for me as a wean. The fields and space were just right for children. We would head out after school and not come back until it was dark. Back then the scheme was new and even to this very day I can smell the freshly-decorated closemouth and the nicely laid out back greens. We called them courts in the auld tenement days but up in The Drum they were back greens or to quote what it would soon become to us weans as *oot the back*.

We moved around Drumchapel as our family increased and decreased. It was common then to swap with someone who had what you needed and you had what they wanted. People lived differently back in those days.

Later, as I got older, I found a lot of people coming to me with their problems. As we all grew up and older we developed and morphed into different characters. Young teenagers would become parents and had to grow up fast and others would soon move, split up, immigrate and others would lose family members. It was just part of life so we all grew in so many ways but The Drum and its community helped us to grow and find our own character in life. There is something very settling about knowing your origins.

I never realized that I was helping people with their problems, I really didn't. I saw people I knew hit the bottle hard and I was the one propping them up. I would offer a sympathetic ear then I would give advice based on my own life story and what I had gone through. On most occasions it was successful but my therapy lessons were not carried out from a leather Chesterfield. We'd sit on a burst couch with half a phone book underneath one end of the bloody thing as a couch leg was missing. It was a symbolic gesture, I suppose, in how the art and act of balancing life was all about for us.

Guaranteed, and I mean guaranteed, all our therapy lessons ended up in tears, a hug and a trip down to the licensed grocers. In The Drum, depositing your tears on someone else's shoulders always tasted better with a half bottle and a few cans.

I have been away from The Drum for many, many years, but I can honestly say without ever being brought up there I would have turned out a lesser human being. I know this for a fact. Some years ago I did learn psychology and did some intensive research on the subject. I got to know really top people in that business and yet I was the one with no papers or certificates. I was asked how could I possibly help (and be successful at it) people with problems and with great ease? I have been asked what is my secret? I have been offered money to tutor my wizardry but I have only one answer as to why I have a good hit rate at helping people with their life problems and situations. It is because I came from a wee scheme in Glasgow called Drumchapel...and I would not change that for the world.

These days I am retired and keep pretty much to myself. I like my private life. There is nothing special about me as I firmly believe that we have, and will continue to have, a big Auntie Madge up every close. That is just one of the reasons Drumchapel is so special and will always be close to my heart.

When I was asked to contribute to The Drum book I had no idea what to say. You have to understand I do not give real names of people I have helped as I always believe in the first port of call in this line of work is securing confidentiality. If people are going to tell me all their worldly life's worries and woes, the least I can do is to keep their confidence in me...well...confident.

I decided that I would allow the creators of The Drum book to use some real-life problem solvers that I have been active with on my column in the Dafty News. Those are all real problems with real people but the names have naturally been changed. I feel this is the best way for me to be in the book without disclosing real people's problems that I helped in Drumchapel. It would be unkind and unfair of me to do that to the great people of Drumchapel who sat on my burst therapy couch.

I use some light-hearted material in my therapy sessions. If we can laugh at a life situation it really helps relax us more and prepare our psyche for the long and winding healing process ahead. I always tell the truth. Growing up in The Drum teaches you that because if you try and con your way you will soon get caught out – and very quickly. The people aren't daft. '

Big Madge on how she defines her style:

I first came across this abbreviation O.C.D. It means *Obsessive Compulsive Disorder*.

I looked intae it and decided, 'Aye, that'll be right.' It should be called F.T.U. *(Fucking Tidying Up)*.

These bams who diagnose people who like things in order are bang out of order, if ye ask me. These poor folks are told they have a disease, even when they are scared tae step oan the crack of a pavement.

So I helped tae develop a cure for this new-age nonsense crap. For those who think they have O.C.D. get yersel' over tae Kansas and walk the yellow brick road and whilst you are at it, play a game of peaver. That'll soon sort yer O.C.D. oot, ya crackpots, ye.

The following are examples of Big Auntie Madge's work (raw and unedited):

Dear Auntie Madge,

I am a keen musician and I have a chance to start a band with four other mates from college. Any tips?

Madge says:

Go solo, son. Paying gigs are hard to get and when you do get them you have to split with the other band members. The best ones are the ones who do it themselves. Bob Dylan must be loaded because he was most probably only answerable to himself, likely. I often wonder how bands like the New Seekers made any dosh and can you imagine being in that band The Foundations? Remember them? They sang that brilliant song *Build Me Up a Buttercup*, way back in the '70s but bugger me, there were loads of them in that band. Imagine trying to split royalties and gig money between that lot? It would be like dividing a giro amongst a highly-populated housing estate.

Have you got a name for your band yet? Seeing as how you're from Glasgow, how about instead of The Carpenters you called yourselves The Jiners and instead of The Whispers how about *Ssssshhhh!*....Don't Tell Any Wan.

Dear Auntie Madge,

I heard that getting a pet makes you more likely to meet someone.

Madge says:

Get a goldfish, sweetheart and stay in the house. Relationships are not worth it. Just think of all the heartache I've just saved you.

Dear Auntie Madge,

I am reaching my 30th birthday and I feel I have not achieved as much as I want to or should be achieving.

Madge says:

Do nothin', son. Live a lazy-arsed life because when you die folks will say you lived a full life anyway so it won't matter a jot.

Dear Auntie Madge,

I think you are naughty to the readers. I am a 21-year-old psychology student and this is not the way to help people who have problems.

Madge says:

See if I was 10, 20, or even 30...months younger Ah would punch your lights out, you cheeky wee bam. See how many folks you can get off the booze or help them find work when you've qualified. Now a way home to your mammy and get your hot water bottle ready and your pyjamas on before I come over there and spank your bare arse. I tell the truth to folks. I don't tell them what they want to hear because that isn't reality.

Dear Auntie Madge,

I think I have an eating disorder. Can you help? I can send you pictures of me before and what I look like now.

Madge says:

Don't bother. Photos of woman with eating disorders always put me off my dinner.
Dear Auntie Madge,

My boyfriend recently asked me if I would take part in a threesome and I was shocked but more shock was to follow when he said he wanted the threesome to include him, me, and my sister. I feel such a mess now and totally disturbed by his fantasy revelation.

Madge says:

Don't worry yersel sick sweetheart. Aw men fantasise about threesomes and aw men fantasise about huvin' it aff wi their partner's sister.

Your sister doesn't even have to be particularly good-looking. In fact, she could be anything from a midget tae a 6ft 2 model; aw men fantasise aboot their sister-in-laws and if they don't huv a sister-in-law they make wan up.

I would call his bluff. Tell him you are on but in one condition: you turn that wee threesome intae a foursome and ask him tae bring his brother.

See if he likes sharing his candy then in the playground.

Dear Auntie Madge

My ex-wife is threatening to take me to court after I said I was going to expose her naked photos on Facebook and Twitter and I might even make a wee video slideshow and put them onto YouTube.

Madge says:

Listen ya wee dafty perv ye. I don't know if you have these photos efter ye became her ex as that would make her the real stupit wan, but if you have a collection of her in the buff when you were married and you have a gripe with her now and want to get her back, ye've nae chance.

I mean get her back in a revenge way. I don't mean get her back as in back together as that would make you even more stupit than ye are noo.

If you ever dare publish they pictures anywhere you'll go straight tae the jile.

I huv yer IP address. I know where you live so wait for a chap at the door coz big Auntie Madge is gonnae be there and you are gonnae be handing me over every single photo you have and if ye don't, I'll be taking care of your hard drive myself, son.

Oh, and if you don't answer the door or you are no in, or even if ye try tae dae a runner, just remember this son…big Auntie Madge disnae need an entrance tae enter a hoose – if you know whit Ah mean?

Oh, jist wan mare thing, normal aunties tend tae gie wee daft boayz a wee dink aboot the ears; am no wan of they daft aunties, I will knock ye flat oot, run ye a nice hot bath then throw ye in it wi a plugged in toaster.

Character
Dougie

Dougie was a fine footballer but he was terribly unlucky with injuries.

He broke his leg in seven places …and one of them was at Dalsetter.

He was also a lazy so-and-so; he was unemployed for so long the benefits office sent him a form and an instruction to go for an interview or they'd stoap his dosh. He went to his local MP claiming he was receiving malicious mail.

Dougie was easy to please. He was content with episodes of Cagney & Lacey, his wife at the Bingo, and a pile of sweety dummy tits fae the van.

Dougie and his best mate Tam were always at loggerheads but feud after feud was never enough to kill their long-standing friendship – they were inseparable.

Their most memorable moment made them household names and a killer punch line now established on the internet…

Dougie & Tam's
Christmas morning encounter with the police:

When Dougie & Tam were both kids growing up in the '70s they both got nice little police peddle-cars for their Christmas; accompanied with pretend radios and of course, nice flashy stripes in the establishment's colours.

As they both played out on the road a real police car drove up containing two officers.

The driver rolled down the window and leaned down towards the little boys and said, 'That's a nice police car you've got there. Did Santa bring you that for your Christmas?'

The wee boys sheepishly giggle and reply, 'Aye, Santa broat us 'em.'

The second cop says, 'That's a nice wee radio you got there, boys. What's your radio name?'

Wee Dougie answers back, 'Mine's Zebra 3, jist like the wan oan Starsky & Hutch.'

Wee Tam pipes in, 'Mine's Z-Victor wan, jist like the motor in Z-Cars.'

One of the cops notices how wide the boys are and decides to play a wee game.

He pulls out his notepad and declares, 'I see you're on the main road, boys, and you don't have any indicators. I'm going to have to book you both for violating the motor vehicles construction and use regulations in accordance with the road traffic law.'

Wee Tam thinks for a minute and says, 'Mister Polisman, who is your car and radio named efter?'

The officer smiles to his assistant before answering, 'Some Like It Hot, after the Marilyn Monroe film.'

Wee Dougie replies, 'And did Santa bring you that?'

Police officer nods a yes.

Wee Tam quips, 'Then, see next year when ye ask Santa for a polis motor and it's named efter a burd; make sure tae tell him the two diddies should be oan the ootside of the motor.'

Dougie on his neighbour:

I'm sure the airlines recruit air hostesses not because of their looks but by their names. I mean, my neighbour upstairs applied to be a stewardess but I told her she's nae chance. Her boyfriend wisnae too happy aboot ma comments tho'. He chapped ma door the other night and said his Sadie was roarin' and greetin'.

Dougie on Tam's wife:

That mad Tam met his wife oan wan o' thawn internet dating agency websites. Tam said he wiz helluva shocked coz in aw these years he didnae think she knew how tae use a computer.

Dougie's granddad:

Dougie's granddad was summoned to the doctor's surgery to be told of his latest tests at the hospital. I have to tell you, Dougie's granddad drank quite heavily for about fifty-odd years, non-stop.

At the surgery the doctor was sad to report that the granddad had cancer and was sorry to inform him of the bad news.

The granddad jumped up, punched the air and let out a scream of sheer delight.

The doctor, bemused, asked why the strange celebration behaviour.

Dougie's granddad replied gleefully, 'I thoat ye goat me doon here tae tell me Ah hud Cirrhosis o' the liver.'

Dougie on his wife:

She's so unlucky, just the other day she tripped over a cordless phone.

Dougie, his childhood, and his maw:

Wee Dougie was outside playing in the street when the ice-cream van came. Dougie shouts up to his window, *'Ma-aaaaaa!* Can Ah get ten pence fur the van?'

His mum opens the third-floor tenement flat window and yells, 'Naw, yer no getting' ten pence, noo away and play.'

There's a queue full of kids at the van.

Wee Dougie shouts up to his window, *'M-aaaaaa!* Gonnae gie me ten pence fur the van?'

Wee Dougie's mother is extremely annoyed. She opens the window and yells down to wee Dougie, 'Ah telt ye naw, noo away and play.'

The van is still there but the queue is getting smaller and wee Dougie is getting a bit concerned. He shouts up to his mum again, *'M-AAAAAAAAAA!!!* Gonnae throw doon a ten pence piece for the van?'

Dougie's mum's temper is set alight. She opens the window and shouts down to wee Dougie, *'Dou-gggglass,* if ye don't stoap yer cerry oan am gonnae huv tae come doon there and belt ye wan.'

Wee Dougie answers softly, 'Well, when ye come doon tae belt me wan, can ye bring me doon ma jumper? I'm freezin'!'

Dougie's wife's ex:

Dougie's wife's first husband left her after twenty-two years of marriage. He said he wanted to be on his own...with the wee lassie that works in the butchers.

Character
Tam

Tam's intro:

Tam doesn't say too much. He can be seen floating around this book but you wouldn't know it. He is one of those characters who have this uncanny ability to make us laugh without even making an effort.

Tam's honeymoon:

Tam and his wife Sandra got married. They booked a nice honeymoon suite in a Paris hotel. When they arrived at the hotel the hotelier asked Sandra if she had any reservations. She said, 'Aye, I don't dae it unless Tam turns oot the lights.'

Character
Auld Betty

Auld Betty was a mixed-up old soul but she was never shy to make an effort in life. She was always at her happiest when she was surrounded by her grandchildren and great grandchildren.

Auld Betty's
Christmas Wish List:

Auld Betty saw a sign at her local charity shop that read: *JESUS SAVES.*

In a flash, she thought that maybe, just maybe, Jesus could help her with her Christmas wish-list. She went home on the bus thinking about the best way to ask the good Lord without being too cheeky. At home she pens her letter...

Dear Jesus,

I'm terribly sorry tae borrer ye but I am a 94-year-old pensioner and I live on my own. I have thirteen great grandweans and I have nothin' to give them for their Christmas this year. I was wondering if ye could help?

I see ye huv some crackin' blouses and denim-gear that wid fit a couple of teenage lassies and I see ye've got second-hand fitba boots; these wid be brilliant fur ma great grandsons.

I wiz wonderin' if ye could oblige me wi the following items:

- Fitba boots in sizes 4 tae 6.

- Blouses tae fit five teenage lassies.

- Denims tae fit ages 12-17 in boayz and ages 5-15 in lassies.

- A bunch of comic books.

- Thirteen jackets tae keep the rain oot in aw sizes.

- Any CDs gone wid be brilliant especially fae that Kylie wan.

- A couple of wee radios, (disnae matter if they come wi batteries or plugs).

- Any auld board games.

- Some warm beddin' fur the younger weans.

- And could ye throw in some trendy wee

- jackets fur the lassies?

Thanks a lot, Jesus.
Signed
Betty

She put a stamp on the envelope and addressed it to: Jesus at the charity shop.

A day later the manageress received the letter and read poor auld Betty's heartfelt plea.

She grouped all her workers together and devised a plan. They wrapped up a big giant parcel and put some goods inside and sent it back to Betty.

Two days later the charity shop received another letter from Betty – again, addressed to Jesus.

The manageress and her staff gathered around the staff-room where they would read dear old Betty's return letter...

It read…

Dear Jesus,

Thanks for replying back to me. I was amazed to get such a quick reply, especially as I know how busy you must be.

I am so happy noo. Ma great grandsons will be able tae play fitba thanks tae the boots. Ma wee great granddaughters will look smart in their new blouses. Aw the tiny weans will be able tae look hip in their new denims. They'll aw be able to read their comics in bed. The smashin' wee rain jackets will keep them aw dry during the wet January. The board games will keep 'em aw busy efter school.

The CDs will keep the weans singing and dancin'. The nice fluffy beddin' will keep the really wee weans warm at night and the trendy jackets will make the aulder lassies feel special.

I huv tae so tho, there wiz nae radios in the parcel.

That's the trouble nooadays, ye cannae trust anybody.

I'd keep ma eye on they buggers that work fur ye in the charity shop.

Merry Christmas and God bless ye, son.
Betty

'When I die I hope tae God it's in the winter time and right in the middle of a hard frost season.'
'Why is that, granny?'
'Coz, I want they grave diggers tae work for their money. When I die they'll need tae earn their crust

wi me, let me tell ye. I'm no gaun in the ground that easily. It will be my farewell message tae the world.

  ~ Betty ~

The Drum:
True Stories

Tiler's embarrassing moment with a housewife:

Apprentice tiler Stevie was working on a new estate and began tiling for a middle-aged couple out in the suburbs. It was a small kitchen splashback, just above and around the newly-built kitchen worktops and units. He managed to begin the task but was in agony with toothache.

He wanted to complete the work but emergency loomed.

He told the woman he would complete the few cuts that were still remaining but would have to come back the next day and grout.

The woman felt sorry for him and offered to drive him to the dentist but he was well enough to make the painful journey to have his tooth seen to.

It turns out the apprentice tiler had to have a tooth removed. It was broken in pieces and had to come out. Even the dentist was climbing the walls.

He returned the next day to finish off the work in the housewife's kitchen.

Worried for the young man, the woman asked how he got on.

'Aye, nae borer. I got a tooth oot.'

'Oh that's great, no more pain?'

'Naw, thankfully.'

He continued to explain his dental journey.

'The funny thing wiz though, when I wiz younger we got gas to put ye tae sleep. These days they jist gie ye a wee jag oan the back of the haun.'

'The back of the hand?' asked the housewife, as she drew an expression and shivered her shoulders.

'Aye, the back of the haun. Here, look, they jag ye right intae that vein and yer gaun.'

The housewife obviously had a phobia about veins and jags and yelled out an almighty shriek but as she did the timing could not have been better. The kitchen was right at the back door and the housewife's husband walked right in off the nightshift to hear her screeching plea, *'Oh no!* Not there, I would rather take it in the mouth.'

Big Peter & His Wee Brother:

'Latin? Who the hell wants tae learn Latin? Are ye aff yer napper?' said Peter's mother.

It was a great chance for Pete to do well and hopefully go on in life. His mother was confused, though.

'Get a real job, like yer father. Ye'll no get very far speaking Latin.'

Pete is not his real name, of course. In the interests of privacy and embarrassment, we've not given him his proper birth name.

Big Peter was like all the kids growing up in Drumchapel. He dreamed of football stardom, meeting a really posh girl from Jordanhill and he liked to go on skiing holidays. Yes, a typical wee Drumchapel boy. Well, the first part applies; all the wee boys played football in the scheme.

His little brothers were not so enthusiastic (although one admitted to having a fantasy about posh girls from Jordanhill, Knightswood and

Bearsden).

'See when Ah get money. Ah'm gonnae meet a burd fae a posh scheme and merry right intae her family. My brother-in-law will be a high ranking banker and my sister-in-law will run me a hot bath and jump right in wi me.'

The younger brother would stay up all night dreaming of meeting his sweetheart who just so happens to have a lot of money.

'D'ye think a toff lassie would be interested in you, ya wee diddy ye? Never mind the money, ye huvnae even hud a bath in a fortnight. Nae wee toff lassie would look at ye sideways, ya daft bastart! In fact, ye cannae even pull at the Argo Centre.'

Of course, not all fathers are as cruel but he did have a point.

'Ya cheeky sod, leave the boy alone.' The mother defended her son. Then tried to reassure him that one day he will meet a smart girl with a secure career and a future.

'Never mind, son, Ah can see ye winching a nice wee lassie fae a nice wee family.'

'Aw, thanks maw.'

'But don't be winching a nurse, son. You don't want merrit intae that. She'll toss ye oot the bed every morning aboot 6am, strip the bed, stretch a clean sheet right across fae one end of the mattress tae the other, then leave a neatly-folded crease at the bottom.'

The father could not control himself from behind his newspaper. It was part of what went on in The Drum. Families didn't hang about and it was great character building.

Big Peter was preparing for a Latin assessment but

was really struggling. His assignment was to write a short story incorporating the Latin words he knew with his own lifestyle and background. He was stumped.

'Fuctifano,' said his younger brother.

'What?' replied big Peter.

'Fuctifano. Just tell yer teacher that's you incorporating Latin wi yer background. It must be a Latin word. It has Latin written all over it. Everybody in The Drum uses that word when they cannae solve a problem or know the answer tae something.'

The younger brother had a point and so did his mother. Who speaks or uses Latin anyway when you are from Drumchapel? Friday night Mass at the Chapel, maybe, but how on earth would you use Latin in your everyday life in The Drum?

The wee brother and his pal knew the answer and came up with some help and ideas for the big brother, Pete.

'Ah've got an idea, Peter,' said the wee brother.

'My pal Frankie's maw did Latin at school and he says he knows Latin. He can help ye with yer Latin assign...thingy...'

Wee Frankie came up to the house and they both locked themselves in a room for about an hour. They emerged from the back room with a sheet of A4 paper and handed it to big Peter.

'There ye go, Peter. A wee story fae The Drum wi Latin words thrown in. Yer teacher is gonna love ye and gie ye an 'A' for this yin. Jist claim it as yer own, nae need tae credit me.'

Big Peter was flabbergasted but his mum and dad were howling with laughter.

The draft read:

Big Tam and his wee fat wife, Angie lived in a council estate with their two children, Chantelle and Tam jnr.

Both parents were prone to participating in some very heavy drinking sessions *(Winus Blooterus)* and occasionally Tam would become a bit agitated and somewhat aggressive and on a weekend evening a barney would break out in the household *(Violentus Domesticus)* and the police would often be called to their home. Tam has been charged a total of eight times for battering his wife *(Assultus Partnerus)*.

Neither Chantelle nor her little brother, Tam jnr would be at home when the fighting breaks out *(Homus Scufflus)* as normally both of them would be outside somewhere.

At times wee Tam jnr would be hanging around with other youths getting high on some substance *(Bucktus Fasticus)* and shouting obscenities to passers by.

Some of the words used were completely offensive and several times the police would be called upon.

Even a normal couple coming home from a simple night on the town would have to pass by the group of youths to yelling abuse like:

'Haw you, ya wanker.' *(Strokus Fingerus)*.

'Ya wee fanny ye.' *(Vaginas Smallius)*.

'Fuck you, ya big arsehole.' *(Intercoursicus, Giganticus Holus Rectumi)*.

And… 'Am gonna dae ye in ya prick.' *(Deflatius Erectus Pricticum)*.

Chantelle would be hanging around the swing park but falsely informing her parents that she was staying the night with a friend *(Lyinus Cuntii)*.

Instead, Chantelle would be getting drunk and

giving line-ups to the local boys *(Ma Turnicus Nexticus)* and four times Chantelle has fallen pregnant *(Upticus Di Sticticus)* but she has had several abortions *(Ridius Di Weanius)* as she cannot afford to bring up a child *(Lackus Doshus)*.

The father of the family was always in trouble and so much so his wee fat wife, Angie; was on tablets for her conditions *(Hysterius* and *Dafti Nervosa,* commonly known as Nervous Dafty).

The father was not much better as he clearly had issues with alcohol and he would spend all the family income *(Giros Fortnightius)* and when he did have some spare money he would blow it all at the local bookies *(Bettus Loserus)*.

One evening the police came to the parents' house to inform them that wee Tam jnr had disappeared and no one has seen him for days *(Fuctus Offtus)* and Chantelle was arrested for shoplifting *(Liftus Propertius)* at the local shopping centre.

A court summons has been issued to all family members and all will appear before a judge over the next coming months.

Already the family have three ASBOs (each) totalling twelve altogether.

Anti-Social Behaviour in the form of:

- Parties *(Loudus Musicus)*.

- Breach of the Peace *(Annoyingus Cuntis)*.

- Selling Illegal Substances *(Profitus Narcoticus)*.

If found guilty the whole family will be locked away with a severe prison sentence *(Bangdus Upus)* and their three dogs *(Bitus Pitbullium)* will have to be re-housed.

The younger brother did meet a nice girl from a posh scheme. Not from Jordanhill but from closer to the city centre, near the West End.

He said it was another world from what he was used to.

He writes:

She invited me back to her house to meet her parents. They were all very nice and well-heeled. The mother was a bit of a snob but I tried to keep my dignity of being a boy from Drumchapel. Snobs were not going to put me off in this life.

I had never eaten like this before. It was a long table. I grew up eating my dinner on the couch with a newspaper underneath to stop me from burning myself. There was jazz music in the background and it was all very restaurant-like…except it was free.

There were so many dishes on the table. I only really knew a pot for stew, a pot for the tatties and a kettle that was always on. This was a banquet I was in. Passing around the food was new to me. I do remember our Christmas dinners when we would have wee plates (that we borrowed) and bowls with the sprouts and all the trimmings of a Christmas dinner.

My girlfriend reached for a deep bowl and asked me what onions I preferred.

I thought there was only one onion: a see-through coloured one.

'No, darling, we have baby onions, wild, bulb. We have them in a variety of colours.'

I had no idea onions came in any colour. If anything the ones I knew were a rusty fawn colour that were always black at the tips for some reason.

My jaw dropped when she bundled a few purple

onions onto my plate. She smiled and said I had a look on me as if I had never seen a purple onion before. I hadn't.

'Wait, are you trying to tell me that you've never, ever, seen a purple onion?'

'Aye, never.'

The tomatoes in the glass bowl looked like red snooker balls.

'And, are you going to tell me you've never seen a red tomato before, either?'

'Aye, but no that bright. Ours were more light red. They didn't shine. Ours looked like a fading paint job on the bonnet of an Escort.'

'But, I bet you've seen a yellow banana,' the future mother-in-law joked.

'Well, actually, no that yellow,' he said, pointing to the bowl on the side unit.

'Surely you've seen and eaten a yellow banana, darling, all bananas are yellow.'

'No up The Drum, hen. Oors only came in two colours: jaundice and black, if you left them too long. If ye wanted shiny fruit aw ye hud tae dae wiz buy a bag of plastic fruit ornaments. They were great for hiding the fitba coupons and the insurance book.

The difference between them was not in class. It was just a difference of upbringing and what they experienced in life. The nice family welcomed the young man into their lives and they spent many years after enjoying the different childhoods. They both learned from each other.

Drumchapel Philosophy:

One night in The Butty pub (poshly known as the

Hecla Arms) a group of factory working men were discussing the latest developments and how they might affect their livelihoods. There was talk of factory closure with redundancies imminent.

It was a difficult time and just at the wrong time for working families: Christmas was just around the corner.

The pints were flowing, as was the patter, and even under the threat to their financial lives, one of the men broke into a tale that had the other men in fits of laughter.

As the storyteller once said of that night: 'It wasn't meant as a joke as such, it was meant as a wee bit of philosophical hope.'

The core of the following is factual, as all things are on The Drum book, but many believe the story is an adaptation of ancient philosophy.

Our philosophical storyteller was quick to make comment when he said: 'This story might have happened in Genghis Khan's days, son, but they can also happen on wee Jinty McCann's watch. It is a true story stretching back many years related to two rival ice-cream sellers.'

An ice-cream van that frequently trawled the late nights in Drumchapel was not a very welcome sight. The locals already had their van and were more than happy. The kids didn't know the difference. This new van had a different musical jingle and was a completely different vehicle model to the one they were accustomed to. This didn't stop the kids from buying their usual liquorice and lucky bags.

The problem was this was not this driver's round. The round belonged to another van. There was no such thing as ice-cream wars back then but there was rivalry all over the city of Glasgow. You have a sprawling housing estate, a large population of children, adults who literally lived off the van, and you got yourself one huge customer base. It is not for letting go.

This story has been passed down so many years but the original drivers are no longer alive. It would have been brilliant to have had their take on it but as the story goes, this is what unfolded…

Regular van versus Stranger van:

The stranger van turned up at closes with a sign in his window:
Buy 20 Marlboro and get two FREE cones

The following hour the regular van turned up with a sign in his window:
Buy two cones and get 20 Marlboro FREE

The next couple of hours went by and again the stranger van turned up at closes with a sign:
Buy 20 Marlboro and get five FREE cones

A short time later the regular van turned up with his latest sign:
Buy two cones and a bottle of ginger and receive your FREE 40 Marlboro

The next evening the stranger van turned up with his brand new colourful sign that read:
Buy 60 Marlboro and get a cone each for every member of your family FREE

Shortly after, the regular van turned up with his new sign in his window:
Buy just one cone and get 100 Marlboro FREE

By this time the stranger van had had enough and confronted the regular van guy.

He said: 'Listen, mate, I'm gonna put you oot of business. Ye cannae keep giving away free Marlboro cigarettes aw the time and expect tae last the distance wi me, pal.'

The regular guy leaned over his counter and said quietly: 'Listen, mate, I've never stocked Marlboro cigarettes in my life.'

The very next day the regular guy secured his run and was never bothered ever again.

It turned out he was indeed giving away free cones as a way of securing the hearts and minds. He would say he ran out of Marlboro and wasn't sure if he would be getting them back in again and that the sign should have been taken down by his young assistant but she forgot.

As long as the locals were getting a free cone they weren't too bothered.

The regular van driver was reported to have said he only sold Benson & Hedges and Embassy because no-one he knew from The Drum smoked Marlboro. They were too expensive.

Tam got suspended from school for questioning the Religious Education teacher:

'How did you get suspended, Tam? You must have said or done something really bad, religious teachers are very tolerant, you know.'

Not Tam's teacher.

Tam said, 'He was giving us aw that Bible malarkey and how Moses supposedly walked across the water. I was 14 and put my haun up and asked him that maybe he didnae walk acroass the watter. Maybe he arrived dead early in the mornin' and walked alang the beach. When the villagers woke up aboot 8am tae take their weans tae school they asked Moses how the hell he got here. Moses then jist pointed tae the sea and said, 'Walked it!''

'I was told by a Minister that God was a man who lived in the clouds and had a long white beard, flowing white locks and holding a crooked staff.

I was also told by a Priest that God was invisible.

Even at a young age I'm thinkin', who the hell sees these things if he's supposed tae be invisible?'

'Sir!' Tam shouted.

'D'ye want tae hear a real Holy story? Wan that is no made up and ye can verify it wi facts?'

'Of course, Thomas, I would be more than delighted to. Please do continue.'

'Cheers, sir, I appreciate it.'

'Right, here goes'…

The Three Wise Men, sir, were actually fae The Drum.

The Three Wise Men were actually totally stupit. There was nothing wise aboot them ataw, sir. In fact, they should have been called The Three Stupit Dafties.

All three had a series of previous convictions; ranging from drink and disorderly, breech of the peace, laundering stolen goods, and all three have been in more courts than Bjorn Borg, sir.

The worst crime of all, however, was when all three

stupit men decided to steal a couple of donkeys after a stag night in Blackpool. It wisnae Bethlehem, but Bedlam.

The Three Stupit Men headed off up the M6 following a daft star in the sky that some mad fortune teller fae the Pleasure Beach said would lead them to the newborn King.

One of the Three Stupit Men, Daft Danny, was a huge Elvis fan so this was his great moment.

The other of the Three Stupit Men wanted to buy more alcohol so they stopped off at the next 24-hour garage, tied the three donkeys up and in went the Three Stupit Men.

Davie returned clutching two large bin bags full of beverages, as wee Shuggy struggled out to the forecourt with cartons of food; namely crisps and sweeties for the munchies later.

However, they were rumbled as they approached Carlisle. It turns oot, sir, that two oot of the three had warrants oot for them and the other was dodging paying his ex-wife's backdated catalogue money.

Whi d'ye think, sir?'

'Thomas, that is disgusting. That is not funny at all. You cannot make fun of the good book, Thomas. Your story is indeed completely ridiculous and swamped with fantasy.'

'How's that, sir? Coz there's nae gold, frankincense or myrrh? Yer right, sir, there wisane any gold, frankincense and myrrh. They had a gold ring that was pawned, dafty Danny is bolted through the neck anyway so that covers him for the Franken…thingy..thing…and the myrrh was Davie's cannabis resin stash he hid under his tammy.'

'Get out of my class, Thomas. A report will be sent

to your parents and the headmaster.'

Tam was thrown out of class for questioning religion. He believed we all have a choice as to what we believe and did not take too kindly to being told something as factual without there being – as he would say – concrete evidence.

He said: 'Don't get me wrong. I am not against religion. In The Drum we had places of worship that were a massive influence and help to the people of Drumchapel but my gripe was one teacher at a Protestant school told me what God was like and he was different to what the Catholic teacher told me. I only asked the question. My wee bit about the Three Wise Men was my way of lightening the load, if you like. It was my ice breaker but it fell back on me and I was chucked out of class for questioning.'

Tam's religious story may not be a positive one but one little boy's place of worship experience is one of those stories that is timeless and still rings in the ears of those who were there and those who heard this lovely story; and brings with it a very positive light and showed what The Drum and its people were about.

Friday night was Mass at St Laurence's Chapel. It was a full occasion with the kids dressing appropriately and they would flock to the Chapel in their droves. Friday nights in The Drum were special. It was the night a lot of people hid from the insurance man.

Just after tea-time the windows of The Drum would open to a loud cry of all the children's names. They were summoned to the house, face washed, and sent to the Chapel for Friday confession.

Most of the names that were called by their parents

were often of Irish origin and you knew by the shout what they were being called in for.

'Gerry! Francis! Sean Paul! Anne Marie!'

Needless to say not many Williams were called. There were of course a few but with the large Irish connection in Glasgow, a lot of the names were adaptations or passed down family traditions. Those Friday nights were mostly about the names fit for a Pope. Paul was a common name but not sure about the Benedicts. That might have gone down a bad road being called something that is easy to rhyme or sounds like.

At St Laurence's Chapel there was no such thing as a divide. All of the community were welcome.

On one Friday night a young boy decided to follow his friends to confession. He got dressed as the others did and off he troddled with his friends.

The friends were regulars to the Chapel. They knew all the words and they knew all the things to do. The other boy had never seen the inside of a Chapel and looked lost. The Priest approached the young boy.

'Are you here for confession, boy?'

'Aye,'said the boy.

'Then what are you waiting for?'

'I don't know whit tae dae.'

'When was the last time you came to confession?'

'This is ma first time.'

'Your first time, really?'

'Aye.'

'And may I ask why?'

The boy was confused and intimidated. The Chapel was full of people, the candles were burning and it was an unusual place for the boy. He only wanted to follow his friends.

The Priest showed the boy what to do. He was calm and very reassuring. The boy soon felt at ease. The Priest showed the boy how to bless himself but the boy got it back to front as he was facing the Priest and was mirroring the Father.

'Ah cannae dae it,' said the wee boy.

'Why not, son? It is really easy. Just copy me.'

'Naw, Ah cannae. I'm a proddy.'

The Priest smiled, took the wee boy to a line of candles and said calmly, 'Why didn't you say so?'

'I wiz scared you'd phone the polis.'

'No, son. Listen. Everyone is welcome in this house. This is God's house and the doors are open to all. You are always welcome in here.'

The Father, to be fair, was brilliant to the wee boy. He was not as strict as the wee boy thought he would be. In fact, years later and into his adulthood the boy said of the Priest and the confession story: 'He was brilliant. I have to say he did not frighten me at all. There were a line of candles and he took me over and said I should just think or even say out loud what was in my thoughts. He was not embarrassed about me being there. The place was really full and he actually brushed me through a line of people worshipping to get to the candles; they all heard me blurt out that I was a Proddy.

It showed then what a great community it was growing up in Drumchapel. There might have been segregation issues and Glasgow has a history of it but that Priest showed that Friday night back in the 1970s that we were indeed all under one house. I am not religious at all and I do consider that roof to be one that covered The Drum: religious-wise or not.

Sadly the Priest's name escapes us all but if he is

alive and reading this book then he has to know he made a huge positive difference to a wee humble boy whose only connection to the Catholic Church was about seven of his friends attended St Laurence's Chapel.

After confession the wee boy and his friends enjoyed a biscuit and an orange juice. For the wee Proddy boy: his snack was on the house; courtesy of the Father, the Catholic Church...oh, aye...and God.'

The Drum:
The Transport

Drumchapel can boast and be very proud of its transport facilities. Technically Drumchapel has its very own train station (Drumchapel) but many still claim a second station (Drumry) which of course is situated in the Clydebank zone; but for Drumchapel residents who lived on the west side of the scheme would get off at Drumry then walk the very short distance across the busy Boulevard to Drumchapel.

Bus routes have been described as one of the best and most frequent. Over the decades Midland and Corporation buses would pick up and drop off Drumchapel residents and visitors. There have been other companies too, no doubt, who would supply vehicles and their service.

Those forms of transport applied more of an interest for adults in The Drum.

For the weans…

Everybody had a shot of a bike in Drumchapel.

Wee Tam, big Tam, Tam's da, Tam's maw, Tam's neighbour and even Tam's dug. We all had some kind of transport that we were either lucky enough to own or we made up through proper childhood improvisation.

In 1973 I rose at 4am on Christmas morning to the most remarkable sight ever and I still haven't managed to remove the shock from my mind and neither do I want to.

It was a ritual for my family whereby my mum would be scuttling around doing the last minute things and so the need for myself and my sister to be out of the house as early as possible on Christmas Eve.

Our dad took us to the famous Kelvin Hall where the annual Christmas carnival took place. I can still smell the elephants and the whizzing sound of the rides. The candy floss and toffee apple aroma filled the high roof and it was just bliss to be a child in that environment.

As ever, we had no idea what was in store for us. All we knew was Santa was coming that night and that reeked heaven for a couple of kids from Drumchapel.

In the weeks prior to Christmas I clapped eyes on a stunning bike that was to become cult in the decades that followed: the Raleigh Chopper.

It was on television and it just looked magnificent. Okay, it was a bit big for me but still, one is allowed to have childhood dreams and ambitions. I only passed comment about how great the bike looked and I never expected to own such a machine, ever.

A couple of kids had a bike and sometimes a bike between a family was enough but Fergie Russell had one and each year at Christmas I can honestly say the kids on our street were treated well by Santa.

At home we had no idea of the time as we were put straight to bed. I am guessing it must have been 11pm but the excitement was just too great. I always nodded off but was still half awake in case I missed something. Each year it was always at 4am when I would get up and waken my sister where we would saunter through to the living-room; eyes half-closed but very excited.

We always had two separate chairs where our toys

would be and the rest of the presents were scattered all over the floor. I couldn't see anything on this particular morning. My view of the presents was blocked by this huge bike. It was the Raleigh Chopper from the television. It was glorious. I wanted to take it out right there and then in the freezing cold and in my bare feet. I didn't care. I remember running my hands over the seat and the seat's back. The metal of the huge frame was shining from the softly-lit lights and the fire was still running one bar. It was Christmas like there was no other Christmas.

That Raleigh Chopper soon became an attachment of me as I was never far from it. The only drawback was we lived one up and carrying that monster of a bike up and downstairs was simply and purely down to the good parents and a good close full of neighbours.

We were lucky in our street as we shared much of what we had. You were everybody's best friend if you had a bike, a good leather ball or a pair of roller skates. Even without those means of transportation we would be creative and think of all ways that could take our backsides from A-Z.

If anyone in the neighbourhood was lucky enough to have new furniture or anything that involved large cardboard packaging we'd make slides out of them by fleeing down a steep hill. Happy days indeed.

Perhaps the most popular, after the bike, was the roller skate and a hardback book…usually an unwanted school book. The foot part of the skate could be altered to fit just about any shoe size and this facility enabled the kids to insert a book onto the skate for seating purposes. All you needed then was a hill and The Drum had plenty of those.

The older kids took part in more dangerous forms of transportation as they would sneak up alongside the dustbin lorry before embarking onto the back or even hang onto the bumper of the ice-cream and groceries van; all without the knowledge of the drivers and co-workers. It was a very dangerous excursion but self-improvisation knows no bounds...especially when you are a housing scheme kid.

In the 60s, 70s and early 80s the tricycle, the scooter, and the base and wheels of an old pram were all means of plaything transport. The kids made the best of what they had and made it work.

'Remember those days when I had a big purple chopper?'
'Aye, and ye hud a bike, anaw.'

Cheeky bastart!

The Drum:
Parties

It is written and engraved in folklore by many people who were there, knew someone who was there, or heard from someone who was there about the most well-known party ever to have graced up a close in The Drum. We are of course referring to the party attended by, at the time, one of the greatest-ever footballers on the planet: the great Hungarian and Real Madrid legend Ferenc Puskás.

Puskás was at that time a universal legend in the game and known throughout the world for his magical left foot and superb goals on the European and international circuit. At that particular time he was neck and shoulders with the likes of Pele and Alfredo Di Stefano. True greats in the game. Legend has it that Puskás ended up at a party in a house in Drumchapel.

Parties around the scheme – for whatever reason they were held – have remained in the *Great Memory* category of many residents. Here we look back at just some true stories from real life people and their incidents. Whether they are memorable for their unsavoury incidents or just their sheer roars of great comedic moments, a story about a party held up a close, through the back or next door cannot ever be omitted or forgotten…

Party Case 1

The name and address of this party case has been reserved to save embarrassment and to respect the man in question as he is no longer with us.

The party was in full swing. An old cliché it may be but the stereo was blasting out tracks from the Bay City Rollers, T-Rex and Patsy Cline. It was a warm summer's evening and the smell of cut grass met the stereo's reverb in the close-mouth. People were dancing and having a great time and in one corner of the room was a man playing skilfully the accordion. In the other corner a neighbour was looking rather worse for wear, as they say. It was clear he had well too much to drink. He wasn't causing any trouble so the folks just left him. He passed out right between the couch and the chair.

The music just kept playing because the stereo allowed you to place a few vinyl records on the centre needle and the arm would manoeuvre to play the next track. It must have been about eight songs before someone noticed the man wedged between the furniture but moves to relocate the drunk man failed as he was extremely heavy and virtually unmovable. Well, he wasn't heavy in the size sense as he was quite a slight man with a thin frame but heavy in the sense that his body was so relaxed the floor and the wedging furniture bore the most of his relaxed frame.

You have to understand that moving a drunk and sleeping man is normally easily enough when you have a party of about twenty-four people but before the party started the host family had arranged the furniture to accommodate the large amount of people that would be coming, going and staying. The display cabinet was emptied of its precious content of glass, fake crystal and ceramic plates bearing the artwork of far away holiday destinations like

Anstruther, Millport and Oban. The cabinet was moved to the back wall but there was not enough space for the couch or the main armchair so the main armchair was moved into one of the bedrooms. The other chair fitted tightly along the living-room wall but almost touching the sideboard and the display cabinet.

The heavy-drunk man was actually in mid flow taking a sip of his drink when he keeled over the arm rest of the chair and got stuck between the feet of the chair and the giant display cabinet. He was so well-hidden no-one noticed; until the pile of records needed to be replaced or put back in their playing stack order. He must have been there for about twenty-odd minutes because eight tracks containing about three-minutes each would result in about half-an-hour.

Oblivious to the man stuck in the furniture the party went full steam ahead until the end of the last record. Panic set in as no-one could actually feel his pulse; he not only fell between the furniture he took with him a cushion that was hanging on the arm of the chair. His feet were sticking out party into the living-room and one of the party-goers, who worked as a nurse, quickly removed his shoes. We have no idea why the man's shoes were removed but they were removed by the woman. She kept yelling things like, 'Circulation,' and 'Breathing,' but later on, it became known she was not a regular neighbour but a friend of a friend of a friend. The whereabouts of the man's shoes becomes clear later on…

All throughout the panic the man was thankfully not dead. He was just completely drunk and fell into a deep sleep. A passing by neighbour, who was not at the party, heard the commotion amidst the scratching of the stereo needle that had played out its last record but the volume was still at its highest level the scratching of the needle could be heard through the open window leading out into the street. It turned out this young man had done some fireman training or some army training of some sorts and quickly came to the rescue. He managed to free the man from the chair legs and the heavy display cabinet.

One of the reasons he was trapped was the flares in his trousers somehow managed to get tucked under the heavy display cabinet. It could only have been as he fell, with his now drunken heavily body, nudged the side of the display cabinet on his way down and the bottom of his trouser leg got stuck under the thick plinth of the display cabinet; trapping him indefinitely.

Twenty-odd people, including a trained exponent and a nurse were what it took to free this man from his capture. In all this time they couldn't waken him, they unbuttoned the top of his Sloppy Joe shirt took off his socks and carried him to the bedroom. With all those people in the room helping; no-one managed to prize his can of beer from his hand. Where he fell there wasn't even a drop of beer and it was freshly opened. He must have sparked the can open, put the foam to his mouth and as he titled his head to take a gulp he fell backwards.

The party-goer who claimed she had trained as a nurse removed the drunk man's shoes, buggered off from the party and was never seen again…neither was the drunk man's shoes. We know this case very well because the next day the drunk man said his shoes were brand new and his wife had ordered them from the catalogue.

Party Case 2

Two couples would often get a wee carry out at the weekend, pig out on crisps and what nots from the van and listen to some hits we now refer to as classics: The 80s.

Both couples were mid teenagers but one of the couples had their own house so the younger couple often went there as it was a place they could get to be together and enjoy the early sweethearts' activities as only young lovers could get away with.

For a long time it was mostly the odd Friday or Saturday night and it would end up in giggles and a lot of young silly behaviour.

On one occasion one of the boys was bursting for a pee but could not get in because one of the girls was using the bathroom herself. The young boy was so desperate he went into the kitchen and grabbed a hold of any container that would accommodate his needs. An empty wine bottle lay beside the fridge. It was the wine the two girls had emptied just a couple of hours before but not wanting to let onto his girlfriend, he pretended he didn't need the toilet as he had just emptied his bladder into a green bottle of 13% blush. Quickly he placed the empty bottle back beside the fridge and even put the cork back on the bottle as to avoid any evidence that may go against him should he get found out. The bottle was dark so you really couldn't see what was in it anyway but without the cork on top the game would be given away. That bottle lay there the full week without being emptied. Both the young couple had forgotten all about the bottle at the side of their fridge. They would have been the first to have thrown it out as they were immaculate and their house was like a palace.

The following Friday both couples go together again for a wee night in complete with Chinese take away and a few cans. The girls fancied wine again and the host girl boasted she still had a full bottle left over from the previous week. She was thinking about the full bottle that lay beside the fridge and believed it was untouched. She confessed she was tidying up around the kitchen area, saw the full bottle, even lifted it up to see how much was left. It wasn't exactly a full bottle but enough to get a stagger. The younger girl poured the contents out of the bottle into a glass and drank some of it. 'It doesn't taste right,' she said. It took a few more moments for it to sink in when the young male host jumped up and said that was the bottle he peed into last week.

It just goes to show you can never judge a bottle by its label.

Party Case 3

One of the best lines ever said actually happened at party in the Drum in 1979 to be exact. Two young men were arguing over music and who was the best artist of all-time and all that important stuff people get into at parties.

One of the guys did not agree and was turning a

little nasty due to the drink. The other guy was cool, calm, and very collective.

The conversation got heated and the cooler guy was beginning to lose it a bit. He said to the other guy, 'Pick a windae, you're leavin'!'

As he looked at the guy after making his threat he realized he had made a huge mistake; the other guy was a big guy and carrying much more weight than the cooler guy, he then changed his mind and continued....'In fact, pick two windaes!'

Party Case 4

There was this man, a visitor to our house, who fell over our coffee table. Okay, nothing strange in a drunken man falling over a coffee table except our coffee table was a tremendous house break-in deterrent. It had huge legs that had round ball-type knots to it and I know how hard it is to fall over one: this coffee table was often my training opponent as I scuttled round the living-room practising the art of dribbling with one of those plastic oranges my mum had as ornaments from the '70s fake fruit bowl.

I was forever whacking my shins and you couldn't get near this coffee table with an army assault unit and a box of matches; it just wouldn't budge and even although the centre of the table had see-through glass *(wait, isn't most glass see-through?)* it was a safe piece of apparatus in our living-room. I used it as goals it was that strong.

This visitor got drunk and fell over the coffee table – tumbling it on its side; wedging the visitor in between the couch and the coffee table. He still had his long coat on and the quarter-length of it – holding two pockets with four cans of beer each – was wrapped around two of the big balls of wood that protruded out to make what I thought was impossible to get near the table.

It took us forever to get this heavy man off the floor. In true Glaswegian style: he fell asleep. If you just came into our house you'd have thought someone gave a silverback gorilla a sedative dart. I say heavy; that's not entirely true in the general sober sense but a drunken man must weigh a ton after he's downed a few tipsies.

In Glasgow a drunken man can wear a coat to a pub to fend off the chilly weather but on his way back from the pub the coat adds about an extra three-and-a-half stone in weight onto it and it has nothing to do with the snow.

The cans of beer in his pocket are wrapped like the crown jewels and no matter how or which way you help him up from the floor he adopts this strange affliction of defying gravity: he always wants to go in the opposite direction. It is always a good idea to leave him lying there until he sobers up. If he is taking way too long then just do your January decorating around him. I hear it is good art. A full brand new carpet cut around a fallen drunk would treat any art gallery in my book. If you pin him up against a wall and support him with two chairs at either side just paint over him. His Colombo-style overcoat housing four fat cans of beer would look great with a '70s kingfisher blue stripe running through him. A sure crowd gatherer and you could charge art lovers the entrance fee into your home.

Party case 5

Garden parties were of the norm back in the 1970s in Drumchapel.

In the summer weekend evenings the locals thought nothing of chipping in for a carry-out and bringing the balmy nights into the star spangling nights. It was common practise. As long as someone got paid, had a couple of quid left over from the Thursday pay cheque everything was game.

In Inchfad Drive they had enough characters there to make a good party with the joke tellers, the singers and the 18-carat bampots. It was the best place for entertainment – according to those who lived in the street.

On a warm July evening Mrs Russell from 68 Inchfad Drive brought out the radiogram and a batch of LP records and singles. The neighbours were quickly drawn to the garden and a small crowd gathered. As long as you brought your own drink, were well-behaved, and could provide some entertainment you were in.

Mrs Russell felt like lifting the party up a bit so she decided to get her hair done as the street guests arrived. One of the younger neighbours at the time, Eleanor Nicol, gave Mrs Russell a makeover with a stunning perm. Mrs Russell already had a thick head of hair but she wanted it shaped and easy to manage and Eleanor obliged.

The party was going well with extra drink coming from young over-18 enthusiasts who ran the errand to the off license in Drumry Road. There must have been a profit in it for their troubles of a can of beer each or even a half bottled shared.

The drink was flowing; the neighbours were all having fun with singing and the infamous story-joke-telling. In fact, the party was going so well Mrs Russell forgot about the tight rollers in her hair. So did everyone else.

The rollers were only supposed to be in for a certain amount of time but that time had passed hours ago.

In full view of the garden party guests Mrs Russell had her rollers removed only to reveal what can only be described as a frizzy afro that made her look like Shirley Temple having an electric shock.

It took days and says before the frizzy hairstyle evened itself out.

The main thing was the party was a huge success.

In The Drum you have to get your priorities right.

*Willie Johnstone from 66 Inchfad Drive and Albert Vernon from 68 were known for their catchphrase '18-carat bampot'. It was a phrase quickly adopted by the weans in the street. If you were an idiot you were simply an idiot but if you were an absolute stoater – you were tagged with the famous 18-carat bampot title.

The Drum:
Oor Wee Street

I have never met so many talented people in such a small area. Inchfad Drive was quite a funny shaped street; almost like a big question mark turned over on its side. The top was shaped in a square that had a couple of streets just off the drive: Fettercairn Avenue and Kerry Place. It was the top end between number 60 and 68 is where the heart of the action was as far as I was concerned.

In fact, those who lived down the hill towards Kingsridge Secondary were often seen at our end as we had so much in front of us and the view was magnificent. Kevin Peddie and his sister Lesley would often hang around number 68 Inchfad Drive. They both had family connections which gave them more reason to as did Willie and Carol Team, who lived in Kerry Place I believe; which was situated right in the middle of both the top and the bottom end of Inchfad.

It was a very tight-knit street where trust was the key in our day-to-day lives. The young lassies were trusted as babysitters and the young guys were often called upon to run an important errand for the elder states people of the street – anybody over 14-years-old was considered responsible and capable of carrying out a basic task like shopping, taking a message to a neighbour, carrying heavy spuds bags up the close or passing a borrow note to anyone who had a spare cup of milk or sugar until pay day.

Only Ants Clarke was given adult-like duties at the age of twelve when he was given watch-out roles for young Stephen Nicol and Fergus Russell as he accompanied both to the putting green at the swing park, farther afield pitch and putt in Knightswood and even a trip to the Anniesland cinema to watch that wee magnificent Volkswagen Beetle character in the film Herbie. A film that change the lives of many a youngster back in the 1970s and a swift rise in toy car sales.

Oor wee street had it all. It was the best street but there are many who can boast the same about their street and each and every one of them will have a point. Billy Savage reckons Kendoon Avenue was the best street. It certainly was packed with more weans at one point than a lot of other streets and like Inchfad it had an array of superbly talented people. Billy's family have a great boxing tradition and not far away lived ex-Rangers star John MacDonald.

It was often thought that major film producers were in Drumchapel to film a four hour epic about Indians, starring Daniel day Lewis on the fields of Halgreen with residents from Kendoon Avenue taking part. As local comedic folklore goes the film was supposed to be titled *The Last of The Monaghans.*

The amount of talent we had in those short-spaced closes was quite phenomenal. We can safely say most of the streets had a bunch of talented people but oor street actually had a band, a karate expert, some terrific wee football players, some cracking singers and of course, throw in a few comedians and you pretty much had a full scale in the entertainments value.

The Vernons from the top floor *(right-hand side looking up)* had the most gifted people. Mrs Vernon was a great singer and any time there was a party, which was very, very often, Mrs Vernon would blast out what she always said was her song: *My Way*. I can still remember Mrs Vernon and her unique way of singing. She always, on every time I saw her singing, always sang in her stocking soles. Even at a young age I remember how her voice would ring and bounce against the living-room walls and the higher pitches seemed to float superbly out of the open window. It was a brilliant place to sing as the reverb was already there for you but you still had to be able to sing and Mrs Vernon could certainly sing. It was many years later when I heard *My Way* on the radio and I remember saying, 'That guy is singing Mrs Vernon's song. I hope he is going to pay her some money for it.'

I grew up believing *My Way* was indeed Mrs Vernon's song. It was a shattering blow to find out it belonged to legendary crooner Frank Sinatra. I doubt Sinatra would be worrying too much because half the world's English speaking population who are into music have probably sang that song themselves and it's a song that has been translated into a hundred-odd different languages but it was up a close in number 68 Inchfad Drive that I first heard that song from a great singer in her soles, clutching a wee hawf; and to me *My Way* will always be Mrs Vernon's song.

As a young boy I was forever asking adults their age. I don't know where this strange habit came from but I thought nothing of it in asking how old they were. Mrs Vernon's age never changed; she was always twenty-one. Maybe being in awe of the people in my street made me want to grow up to be like them and if I was 8-years-old and a neighbour was old enough to tell a joke and get a laugh I wanted to know what age they were so that when I became his or her age I too could tell a joke like that. Mrs Vernon was always twenty-one and you know what? when I think about it now she probably was always twenty-one. She brought so much life to the neighbourhood with her talented vocals and was always the first to call on if you wanted entertained.

Her husband, Mr Vernon, was also a very talented man. I remember him greatly with his jokes. He was always telling jokes; a real joker-in-the-pack but he could also sing. It was common for both Mr & Mrs Vernon to sing one after the other at parties and the so often get-togethers.

Mr Vernon worked as a carpet fitter for many years and worked for a company in Helensburgh. He left way early to see him take the journey down the broken path and alongside the school fence at St Laurence's Primary but on his return he was a welcoming site for the kids. You could see him come over the little hill on his way back from Drumry train station. He had a special walk that was instantly recognizable from even a great distance. As he approached the side fencing at St Laurence's we would all run down to meet him. He was a strong man and would lift all of us up, put someone on his shoulders; a couple around his waste and the rest of us would just hang onto his legs. Of course, the reason we did this was he brought sweeties from the caravan that was parked in Drumry Road which would now be directly across from the Chinese take away. We would hang upside down pretending we were looking for a swing but we were actually fiddling inside his pockets for loose change. He knew this, of course, and played a long with it. He would purposely put coins in his pockets so we would find them.

The caravan burned down years later but it was just a little caravan that sold the necessities in life: sweeties, fags and the papers. Mr Vernon was an exceptional man and very well-appreciated in the neighbourhood. Recently he became the last neighbour legend to pass on. Even now when I see or feel loose change I think of Mr Vernon's pockets that he would jingle and torment the weans before giving us all a reward with enough to buy sweeties at the wee caravan.

The Vernons had a very tight family comprising of Brain, Stuart, Stevie, Catherine, Sandra and Lynne. Stevie and Sandra were twins. Actually, in between the tight close space there was also another set of twins but we will get to that shortly. The girls were all up for entertainment; what a crowd they were; absolutely hilarious and babysat for me on many, many occasions. Sandra once said that she loved to babysit for me and my wee sister but not because we were good kids; it was because our mum worked in Beattie's biscuit factory and she often brought back the scraps from the factory like broken biscuits that probably never made it past quality control. In the end, growing up as a wean in Drumchapel in the 70s – a biscuit was a biscuit no matter what condition it was in.

The boys were great lads and were very kind to the younger street members. Stevie was the one who was in the band. Music it seems was big in the Vernon's household and you could see why they were a talented bunch. They were indeed The Partridge

Family of Drumchapel.

*'It was a shattering blow to find out the song My Way
did not belong to my neighbour but in fact international
legend Frank Sinatra. Then again, it was partly my fault
for looking too much up to the elders in my
neighbourhood. They were like superheroes to me but
idolizing has a funny way of backfiring and no more so
than when I always heard the name Nat King Cole being
mentioned in just about every conversation that popped
up. Years later when I left school and started work I was
soon to find out he was actually a singer.'*

The Wee Shop (Inchfad Dr):

The real date is explained in the book but to give you
the basics of it; here is a little, little something that
might surprise you.

The plan and foundation was actually started in the
summer of 1974 but for some reason the shop didn't
start trading until much later (1975 is near the mark).

Proof of the foundations in 1974 is stamped on a
very special day: July 7th, 1974.

On this very day West Germany played Holland in
the World Cup final.

Everybody in the street were rooting for Holland
except for one family in particular – the Grants.

Gerry, Mark, Thomas and the twins Barry and
Lynne, had German family connections and so it was
only fitting they should support West Germany.

Mark, Thomas, Barry, Lynne, Fergie Russell and
some others (*possibly Louise McClements*) all played
between the hole where the shop was to be built and
roller skating down the adjacent path towards the

power station. Well, it wasn't roller skating in an upright position; they had hardback books like The Beano where they positioned the book on top of the skates and used as a wee 'hudgie'.

It was a gray but quite balmy day prior to kick-off. Thomas and Mark were screaming down the path in Lynne's skates chanting *DEUTSCHLAND! DEUTSCHLAND!*

Some of the kids thought they were on Holland's side as it sounded like DUTCHLAND! DUTCHLAND! But the Grant family gave the confused kids a lesson in foreign vocabulary and we still say to this day that fitba is the greatest-.ever geography lesson.

We tried to find the original builder of the shop to find out the exact opening day but time, people and records are hard to come by as there wasn't much technical data stored in those days.

The foundation was a hole with lots of sand *(hence the attraction)* with planks of wood for support. This is what makes us believe it must have been the foundations of the shop because it couldn't possibly have been anything else.

Some conflicting stories claim the foundation was actually started by the factors where a new close was set to be built but those reports have been rubbished. It must have been for the shop only.

On my annual pilgrimage to The Drum I was shocked to see my old street completely revamped. Gone were the old closes replaced by neat rows of wee terraced houses and plant pots.

The shape of the street remained the same with its sloping down towards East but because of the rebuilding the new house numbers just didn't match their original positions.

Number 68 Inchfad Drive is now where 66 used to be. 66 is now where 64 used to be and 64 is now where 62 once stood.

I was telling my old neighbour, who lived down the stairs from me, about the new formation of Inchfad Drive.

He said: 'Aye, I know, since we left, that street has went doon hill.'

*Inchfad Drive was not only famous for its great people but there is a song, titled Inchfad Drive, from the brilliant album titled, Inchfad Drive, by Johny Corrigan. The album is a highly recommended listen and available on iTunes.

Oor Wee Street by Carol Fergus:

We lived in Invercanny Drive. I fondly remember the high flats where many a time we could be found playing on the cube-shaped thing that had a high swing and monkey bars on it. No rubber floor then; if you fell off then you would end up with bruises and scratches; but did that stop us? No way, it was a great piece of equipment to play on.

We also used to get large cardboard boxes from Presto down the shopping centre and then use them to slide down the hill at the high flats. What a laugh we used to have.

There were also the bars, halfway down Invercanny Drive that ran up beside St Pius, up to Cally Avenue. We spent hours twirling round and round those things.

Drumchapel was a place where you grew up making the best of what you had. You made some great friends and you also got into some fights.

Sometimes people got called a snob if they were a bit better off than others, but everyone was the same; this is why we all lived in a housing scheme.

The best thing, for me, was that everyone would stick together to protect their own; not afraid to stand up for themselves. I feel that this is what Drumchapel gave me and I wouldn't change it for the world.

Oor Wee Street by Kirsty Ayre:

I lived on Dunkenny Road until we moved to Halbeath.

I remember the telephone box at the top of Halbeath, which was right outside my house.

My mum told me one day the army was called out because there was a 'suspicious package' found in the phone box.

They shut the street but mum and all the neighbours were watching from the window. The army brought out a wee robot to check it out and it blew it up with a controlled explosion – turns out it was a shoe box with nothing but empty cans in it.

I also remember going to a club every Friday night in the United Free Church on Dunkenny. It was called the King's Club. We used to play games and learn about religion.

I also had lots of fun days out.

I've remained friends with most of the people I met there.

Brilliant memories of playing in the fields beside it, which was always overgrown, and made for a great game of hide-and-seek by just diving into the grass.

I actually still have the bible I was given at the King's Club!

Remember the rag man? He used to stop on Dunkenny Road.

One day when I was a kid my mum and dad had bought me a very expensive red coat. When the rag man came I traded it for a plastic ring – which I was over the moon with.

When my mum asked where I got it and I told her, she went mental.

My dad drove all over The Drum trying to find him, needless to say he was never found.

Oor Wee Street by Mags Shovelin:

I Remember going for shopping at the vans that parked in Fettercairn between Katewell and Inchfad.

There were also Hayburn Dairy and Colin Campbell, the fish van.

Also, does anyone else remember the day one of the light poles in Fettercairn fell?

Oor Wee Street by Margaret Savage:
Living in Never, Never, Land

When Stephen Nicol asked me for a photo of myself from the seventies I had the dilemma. I didn't have one. Did that mean that I didn't exist? No, it meant my parents didn't have enough money to afford a camera to take a snapshot of our hand-to-mouth existence.

To be honest, this has never caused me any concern. I never knew we didn't have money. You don't miss what you've never had.

Okay so sometimes my mother covered the telly with the table cloth and swore she didn't have a TV, or hid behind the sofa when the rent man peered through the letter box. But when you are a child it's all just a big game. We had a coin gas meter which was rusted inside because the frozen coins had melted…a trick from plasticine and 10p's…*(another story)*.

The heading at the top may suggest I had a fairytale existence; that I flew from the wardrobe with wings at my feet, *(well, I did but that's another story)*. But no, this is not a JM Barrie story, this is Glasgow *Never, Never,* which I am sure many will recognise, and if you don't, well I guess you never had to dodge the lecky man or pawn your good suit.

My *Never, Never,* started with the Provident woman *(pronounced Prawveee wumin).*

She was this strange woman that shuffled into our flat and produced the golden ticket. It introduced me to confidence and delinquent charm. I had to visit every shop and shout from the doorway, 'Do ye take Provee cheques?' ignoring everyone already being served, ignore the sly looks from the shop assistants and generally leave with a smile on my face.

Provident cheques were a credit agreement with retailers and my mother paid back tenfold: both with cash and dignity.

When my mother passed away she still owed £25. I

told the Provident woman where to go, and her parting words were, 'Yer mother would be ashamed.'

I bet she is laughing at the Bingo in the big hall as I type.

We also used to visit the pawn shop in Clydebank. This to me was a complete mystery. Everything was very cloak-and-dagger. The parcels were all wrapped up in brown paper and string. Everything covered in dust with a wee man peering from behind a grill with an apron and small glasses on.

My nose would twitch with unfamiliar feelings (I always was a strange one).Bewitched had a lot to answer for. I digress.

All I knew was my mother handed over my dad's suit, my brother's fishing rods, and even her wedding ring; and we had more food on the table that week. I also knew I was never to tell my father, who worked away at the time.

Finally, there was Carlo, our ice -cream van man.

Every now and again my mother would call me in from my adventures as a Superbeing to take a note to Carlo.

The ice-cream van had arrived in our street and it was more popular than a Radio Clyde Road Show. I was given a note – which I never read, to this date, I don't why, maybe I knew I didn't want to know what it said. I have always had Superhuman instincts.

I handed it over. He gave me an exasperated look but as a child that means nothing, as an adult it means failure.

Thank God I was crap at body language as a child otherwise I would have grown up with an even bigger inferiority complex.

Anyway, I gave Carlo the note, he gave me: 20 Capstan Full Strength; one bottle of orange; one bottle of Irn Bru; one Cardbury Fry's Cream; one packet of Askit powders, and a 20p sweetie mixture. What does that say about my childhood? We had rotten teeth, my mother had a constant headache and died of cancer.

Would I change it? Not or all the clapping of hands to make a fairy live.

Oor Wee Street by Michelle Stewart:

The best years were the 80s.
   Growing up in Drummore Road, so many happy memories growing up there, and so glad I did.
   All the kids in the street played together and the games I can remember were: kick-the-can; Double Dutch skipping ropes, and having a big ghetto blaster on at the front and dancing away; and when it was raining we would play wee schools up the close or swap scraps.
   I can always remember my gran telling me that Billy Connolly often came to visit his family who lived on Kinfauns, which was not far from where we stayed.

I went to Pinewood Primary along with my sister and this was a good wee school. We never seemed to be late as it was right across the road from us.
   The school also had a memorial garden for the Girl Guides that were sadly killed in the bus crash 17

years ago past in September. They have now set up a lovely garden at near by Camstradden School; which the local people put a lot of their time and effort into, to make it a place were you could go to ponder those thoughts.

My best friends were Sheena, who later left and went to live up in Stornoway, Suzanne McLean and Rhona Thomson; all at the time of school in the 80s. Though with the help of Facebook have found many more from The Drum since moving away in 1985.

My mum, like myself, saw an add in the local paper looking for memories of people growing up in Drumchapel and surrounding areas, and she thought she would send in a picture of the street party that Gairbraid Avenue Maryhill had when the Queen was made to the throne.

So, mum posted it away and got word back from the author of the book in the add to say he would forward a book on to her once it was printed.

A few months later the book came in the post and mum was looking through it and came across two very unusual pictures, of which left her speechless.

The first was the house which was built in a week and known as the 7-day house. This house was what my dad and his family had bought in the 50s (Switchback Road) after winning the Littlewoods Pools, from their house in Katewell Place in Drumchapel.

We had never before in our life seen a picture of it before, till the book.

Then the other picture was the dancing days in the

50s/60s. It was a competition and mum and dad were in the picture dancing away. Again, it was a picture that both could not get.

Sadly, mum Passed away in 2010 and I know she would have loved to have seen this book.

I would be touched if it could be in the book.

Mum`s name was Isobel Stewart and my name when growing up there was Michelle Stewart.

Oor Wee Street by Neil Henderson:

I lived in Drumchapel between 1962 to 1980.

I lived in Carolside Drive from when it was built and remember my mother telling me about how the decision was made who got what flat in the close.

All the keys were put in a builder's bucket and each person stuck their hand in the bucket and what ever keys you picked; that was your flat for the next twenty years.

My mum got a top flat but she wanted a bottom flat with a garden so swapped with a future neighbour who didn't want the hassle of looking after a garden.

Simple. They became good friends as did the rest of our neighbours.

We had back court concerts using the clothes poles washing line and sheets to create a theatre which could rival a King's Theatre Variety Night.

Every summer we built a dookit and had to guard it with our lives to avoid rivals stealing oor doos and against the cleany coming to pull it down when we were at school.

We set up a Sentry shift system the Romans would

have been proud of.

Oor Wee Street by Stevie Bryceland:

As a kid I worked in Jackie Dickie's ice-cream van, that used to sit at the corner of Lochgoin Avenue and Achamore Road. This would have been from around 1970 to 1972.

My tasks were to serve the weans sweets like gobstoppers, penny carmels, MB bars etc, and I got paid the princely sum of a half crown for my efforts.

Everything was going great until the country changed to decimal currency and I could only count in old money. This led to a steady stream of angry weans and parents at the van complaining that I had short changed them, much to Jackie's displeasure *(he could be a grumpy sod at the best of times)*.

So until I grasped the new money I was confined to filling the shelves and making cones.

Best part about the job was getting broken chocolate bars for free, and I can assure you there were plenty, as it was me who was opening the boxes and filling the shelves.

I stayed at 4 Lochgoin Avenue and went to Lochgoin Primary at the time.

68 Inchfad Drive (front)

68 Inchfad Drive (side)

The Drum:
You Taking the Biscuit?

The waff of chocolate biscuits could strip the nasal hairs off an Alsatian dug. Beattie's biscuit factory was famous for biscuits but also for spreading a much-welcomed aroma around parts of Drumchapel.

At the height of its flourishing empire *(no pun intended)* Beattie's was a thriving factory where many large numbers of women and men would gather from parts of Drumchapel and surrounding areas. Some travelled longer distances but nearby Knightswood, Yoker and Clydebank were hot places for Beattie's workers.

Alongside Great Western Road you would see shifts coming and going from factory floor workers, cleaners and administration staff. The large gates were busy as any large factory with the amount of HGVs leaving with their sweetening cargo to their return for pick-ups.

If you lived in Heathcot Avenue or Heathcot Place you were the first to get sniff of the nice biscuit smell as the factory ventilators let free the magnificent aroma. If you stood at the top of the field in Heathcot Ave you could see the many white overalls and wee nylon white hats as shift workers went about their out-of-factory duties like emptying the bins or sneaking out for a quick fag on the sly. In the summer the workers would use their breaks to bathe in the large grassy surroundings within the factory gates and roars of laughter could be heard from mid to late afternoons as the workers were clearly enjoying the sun, the break and the getaway from the rigours of biscuitry.

The factory workers also housed many a great social night. Whether it was an end of term party, someone leaving, a birthday bash, Christmas or just an excuse for a get together, the factory workers were never too shy to let their hair down.

In one of Billy Connolly's famous LPs from the 1970s, the Big Yin was making a gag and referred to a bus going to Drumchapel. In the LP you can hear loud roars of approval from a group of women – obviously from The Drum – but those women were part of the Beattie's biscuit factory night out on the town. Their applause was welcomed by others in the audience as Billy Connolly also spent part of his life in The Drum.

Parties were frequent back then. People worked hard but rewarded themselves at the weekend with a treat, a well-deserved earner for their weekly troubles sweating over hot plates, underneath grinding wheels and hacking it out on factory floors all over the area.

Sadly, when the factory closed many lost their livings and for many others their last and only perspective in life as they were a bit older and when the economy collapsed and changed the faces of housing schemes in and around the Glasgow, The Drum suffered dramatically. However, when anyone talks about the biscuit factory you cannot help but cast your mind back to that wonderful smell that coated the air of Drumchapel.

The annual Christmas night out had come. It came

just at the right time. Many of the workers had worked the whole year and this was their night. It was also a fruitful time for the babysitters as the amount of workers heading out to their glitzy event would be parents or a parent of young offspring.

Two young children, Stephen and Karen, were being looked after by the lovely Helen Rankin. Helen, as described often in this book, was a teenager who was full of life and was very popular in the community. At this time of year it was extra special to be full of life. The Christmas trees lit up the scheme, the cold snap that brought the now famous orange glow from the street lights, and the magical sound of Christmas songs blasted from the radio. The only drawback was the Beattie's night out was during a school week.

It wasn't Helen's work to get our school clothes prepared. That was the role of the parent(s) and guardians. It was the last babysit of the year. Helen would have the full run...including the biscuit tin...and she was paid a wee bit extra as it was Christmas. Everything was just as it should be.

The night had gone in a slash, as the kids were enjoying themselves. They didn't hear the parents coming home from the night out. They were totally sound asleep, oblivious as to the awakening world.

The clock said 8:50am. It should have been 7:50am so either the clock was wrong or somebody has slept in. It was the latter.

In a rush the older kid, Stephen, got up and scrambled around for his school clothes. They were not on the end of his bed and they were not even in his room. The younger kid, Karen, got up and was so used to the morning ritual of having clothes at the foot of the bed, hanging over the two posts.

'Where's ma jumper?'

'Where's ma cardigan?'

'There's no even any socks.'

The boy had gone quietly into the parents' room and asked where the school clothes are.

'We've nothin' to wear, mum.'

Both the mother and the father were sound. Not a cheep. The Beattie's night out had been a great night but to the cost of sleeping in for the kids.

This was a one-off. It has to be said the two kids were more than well brought up and this occasion never happened before and it has never happened since. It was one of those great nights that went on a little longer and they didn't get in until well late.

The mother opened one eye and said to her son, 'Just put anything on. It's the last day of school anyway. The teachers won't mind.'

'Can we wear anything we want, mum?'

'Aye, just wear anything today. I slept in.'

That was enough for the boy. It was carte blanche time. Time to kick it up a few notches. It was time to impress his school mates.

The school was strict on uniform but did look away if the pupil didn't wear one. In Drumchapel not everyone wore a school uniform but appropriate dress sense was always encouraged. Some families were too large and uniforms were not cheap. Some schools provided the basics but blazers, shoes, shirts, trousers, skirts et cetera were oftentimes more expensive than casual clothing. There were some provisions and support but the school authorities knew the economics of a sprawling housing estate and so this was a reason some schools were quite okay about the full uniform. Other schools (and it was mainly down to what some teachers preferred) were more strict than others.

It wasn't uncommon to wear a shirt and school tie but casual skirt or trousers. A couple of kids heading to school at 9:15am dressed quite casually would not attract any attention.

However, young Stephen and Karen were not in their uniform, as it wasn't ironed or prepared, and they were not even dressed too casually.

Some weeks prior to the Beattie's Christmas night out, both Stephen and Karen had pantomime evenings to attend. They were forbidden from wearing their new clothes until the pantomime night at a theatre in Glasgow. This was a chance to take the mother's words to heart, 'Just put anything on. It's the last day of school anyway. The teachers won't mind.'

The two kids walked to school, knowing they were fifteen minutes late, it wouldn't have mattered if they were twenty minutes, or even an hour. As far as they were concerned, and as far as the teachers would see; they were late and that was it.

They sauntered to school without a care in the world. Some adults in the street did give the kids a second glance. They were not dressed for school.

The boy had a brightly-coloured pullover on with The Wombles plastered all over it and an Afghan jacket left at the house by his uncle; the tail of which trailed the frosty ground. He had a pair of bell-bottom trousers, reserved for the pantomime night, and a pair of football boots on…screw-ins. Can you imagine that journey to school on an icy ground? No wonder it took them about an hour to get to the school.

The girl was kitted out in a pair of blue silk flared trousers that were tucked into high boots. A floral shirt with a fake fur coat draped over the shoulders and her long blonde hair sticking out of a beanie hat.

Well, the mother did say they could wear anything.

Two police officers drove past the kids for about 100-yards then stopped, obviously thought for a moment then did a 3-point turn and drove slowly alongside the two kids as they walked on the grass verge.

There were questions asked before one of the officers spoke into his radion

He said: 'I've got one half of ABBA here. I'm gonna need assistance to find the other two.'

The kids tried to explain to the officers about the Beattie's night out, the dancing babysitter, all the caramel cake they ate, sleeping in for school, and the need to get to school quickly before all the good presents are handed out.

The officer said: 'Are you two takin' the biscuit?'

Fortunately the police and the school enjoyed the funny side and in fairness, so did the parents. A quick escort back to the house and a change into proper clothing and all was forgotten about.

As local legend would have you believe, the now famous childhood biscuit joke is said to have come from Beattie's biscuit factory but to be honest, as much as the joke is still an iconic moment from the school playgrounds to the close-mouths, the joke was most likely originated from someone else and from somewhere else…

'Did you hear about the fight in the biscuit factory?

Well, two *Bandits* hit a *Penguin* over the heid with a *Club,* tied them up with a *Blue Riband,* before making their *Breakaway* in a *Taxi.'*

The Drum:
Nothing Sells Better Than Hope

When we have nothing our hope levels rise quite considerably. As young kids we tend to look up to adults in the hope they can save us. They never lie – right?

Wrong.

I was lucky enough to be surrounded by good honest people. My family, relatives, and neighbours. However, on one particular day I stopped looking to stranger adults to bail me out or help me with a solution. I just stopped believing in stranger adults and here's why.

I was a very young boy when it was announced the Scotland versus England game was to be shown live on our screens. We had our colour television set since the previous year's World Cup and this was the first live game in my own house since then. I had always been downstairs watching live games in the Russell's house. Saturday was going to be great

A close friend of my dad was Tommy Jeffrey. The Jeffrey family lived in Abbotshall Ave and coincidentally we all met up again some time later when both our family and the Jeffrey family moved to East Kilbride.

Tommy was the same man when I was a child as he was when I became an adult. He was honest, a decent man indeed, and very funny. Always a pleasure to be around. He was the perfect host and entertainer. He knew most and everyone knew him. On this particular day he brought with him a guy from the pub that he actually didn't know that well.

There was myself, my dad, Tommy Jeffrey, and this other guy whose name escapes all of us. Apparently he was the last one standing in the pub with nowhere to watch the live game. Tommy, or Uncle Tommy as he was affectionately known as, felt sorry for him and brought him along. My dad approved. Tommy didn't hang around dafties so if Tommy said the guy was okay then that was good enough for my dad.

To be fair, the stranger was actually an okay guy. He wasn't drunk, he wasn't loud and he wasn't a a hindrance at all. He just changed my way of thinking about stranger adults from this day on.

As we sat down to watch the game my dad took his usual pole position with his 'father chair' and Tommy sat beside me. The stranger guy sat on the other seat. It was a typical Scottish football atmosphere with a few cans on the table, a couple of halves and crisps and juice for me. It felt great. It was as close to a New Year's party as you could get – except there were nae wummin.

We all fancied Scotland to win. In fact, according to my research Scotland were actually the favourites going into the game. Scotland started off well. They hit England a few times and it looked like we were going to 'murder them'. A phrase often heard from drunken supporters.

The confidence was high and to be honest we never had any feeling of being in danger until Gerry Francis picked up a Mike Shannon pass and hit a sweet shot from way outside the box. 1-0 to England, after just a few minutes. I was gutted. My dad was raging at our goalie as he never even moved.

We still never felt in any danger. The stranger guy

leaned over to me and said: 'Nae danger, son. We'll beat them 2-1.'

Not long after, England's Beattie scored from a header, after Kevin Keegan had about 25-yeards to run wide without a single challenge. 2-0 to England.

The stranger guy leaned over to me and said: 'Nae danger, son. We'll beat them 3-2.'

I believed him. How could I not? He was calm and reassuring and wasn't any trouble at all. I think now the only reason Tommy Jeffrey brought him to our house was because he was lonely and maybe too quiet. Tommy was a kind man. He had a very nice family and was a really nice guy so I can imagine Tommy feeling sorry for this guy in the pub.

When Derek Parlane hit the post I started to believe this guy even more. I was thinking, maybe we *will* beat England 3-2 but I knew myself how difficult it was as our games of football down at St Laurence's pitch were always about goals, comebacks and numbers. When you are two goals down it is quite a challenge to claw that back.

England's Gerry Francis orchestrated another as it broke to Bell who struck a decent shot from outside the box. I am not sure if our keeper Stewart Kennedy could be blamed or if the shot was that good. Either way it was now 3-0 to England.

The stranger guy leaned over to me and said: 'Nae danger, son. We'll beat them 4-3.'

I actually believed this was possible. Scotland did have spells where they could have and should have scored. My faith in this stranger guy lit up. Scotland were awarded a penalty. I was thinking, maybe we can beat England 4-3. Maybe this could be the first gal of many. The dream was very much alive.

Bruce Rioch stepped up and slotted the ball past Ray Clemence with ease. It was now 3-1.

The stranger guy just sipped on his can as my dad and Tommy jumped for joy. The stranger guy just winked at me like a likeable cold assassin.

We had an open goal chance but Duncan hit the side netting, just inches from the post. Even at 3-1 down we actually were unlucky.

Keegan intercepted a poor pass from Tommy Hutchison in the middle of the park and did what he always did really well and that was running at defenders. He won a free-kick just outside the box. Again, that man Gerry Francis scored from an indirect free-kick.

4-1 to England.

For us it was all but over. No team can come back from that deficit. We were just so far behind and Stewart Kennedy was having one of those bad days.

The stranger guy leaned over to me and whispered: 'Nae danger, son. We'll beat them 5-4.'

I have no idea if he was trying to mask my disappointment or he genuinely believed Scotland could make a comeback of that magnitude. The funny thing was, I still believed him. He was that convincing.

Finally, England score a fifth goal after a scramble that began with England hitting the crossbar then the post before Johnson put it away to seal one of the most disastrous score lines in my, or any other generation.

Throughout the game I looked to this stranger guy

for some much-needed hope. I looked up to him not because he had any knowledge of the game because I probably had more than him, even at that age, but he was calm and cool and he never raised his voice. Where I came from they would say he was neither up nor doon.

I looked to him to see what his reaction would be. Surely he was not going to say, 'Nae danger, son. We'll beat them 6-5.'

He didn't. He just leaned over and said: 'Next time, son, next time.'

I never trusted a stranger guy again. I looked to him for hope and to help us beat England like he was a messiah. More fool me. He was indeed just a guy from the pub. The worst type to put your nail-biting worries in front of for a cure or a fix.

Nothing sells better than hope. I found that out as a wee boy growing up in The Drum and watching a game of fitba.

Wembley: the revenge

In 1977 Scotland defeated England at Wembley 2-1.

As many of you will remember the Scottish fans took some memories home with them of the famous victory. Some were fortunate enough to cut a piece of the goal net away but most of the fans cut up some Wembley turf as a souvenir.

After the hysteria and the high died down some fans started to flog the hallowed turf for anything from the price of a pint to a deposit on a Ford Cortina.

There was a gentleman reportedly from nearby

Clydebank trying to sell his Wembley turf in the Drumchapel area. There were no takers, however, and the hustler was finally rumbled – not by the police – but by an eagle-eyed pensioner resident of Drumchapel who just happened to be a member of the Drumchapel Bowling Club.

As the hustler laid out his 'Wembley' turf on the pub table for exhibition and sales pitch purposes, the sharp-eyed pensioner fumbled under the table for a few moments, making clattering noises, before producing a small white hard ball.

He placed the ball on the square-foot green that was encased inside a low lid box, put on two pairs of glasses; examined the turf before declaring: 'Ach, away tae buggery, son. That's no Wembley turf. That's a clipping fae oor green near the ditch end.'

The very next day the green keeper at the bowling club was seen patching some fresh turf together at the ditch ending, knitting it neatly into the sparse square patch, mumbling, 'They bloody rabbits must huv been here last night wi a cake knife and a straight edge.'

The Drum:
St Laurence's Pitch

S t Laurence Primary school had its main gates at Kendoon Ave but you could access the school from Halgreen and Inchfad. During school days the kids would enter through the gates but at weekends, because of the gates being closed, they would jump the fence or go through many of the gaping holes in the wired perimeter.

The school was fairly large in size and had a number of areas to play and hone some developing skills; especially if you played football.

Near the power station there was a small gate entrance to the school. This was situated at the foot of the two Inchfad paths and comprised of two gate entry walls. One wall in particular, the highest of the two, played host to a game called *Best Man Fall.* This was where one boy or girl would stand on the wall and say how he or she wanted to die. Now, it wasn't a real game of death but you could choose a grenade, knife, bullet or even a rock to the head. Of course, these were imaginary weapons. The rest of the group would stand waiting on their turn in front of the wall and one person would be nominated to carry out the imaginary execution. Probably these days a play act like this would be banned but honestly, there were no weapons or even anything resembling a weapon was ever held in any kids' hands. It was the act of throwing a weapon and the act of receiving a weapon that was the trick. Just good old-fashioned honesty-to-goodness play acting without any props.

The winner of the game would be the ones who did

the best fall from the wall; hence the title *Best Man Fall*. The title was never changed to accommodate any girls who wanted to take part; it was simply called *Best Man Fall*. Most of the falls were copies of what the kids saw on television. The *Six Million Dollar Man* and *Combat* was a favourite back then to get some falling ideas and the area of St Laurence's Primary was just one of those great places to carry out some early acting skills.

Like most things back then the kids didn't receive any lessons or coaching. Sure, kids did play football and received guidance from managers and coaches and any kid taking part in group sessions did receive lessons of such in regards to their craft or art but most of the stuff was learned by watching the stars and carrying out those acts in the school areas and play fields around the scheme.

Some older kids gave up their time to teach the smaller kids some crafts. Helen Rankin was a great example of this when she taught dancing at night in the main hall in St Laurence. The class Helen took was a huge success and many, many young girls in the area all flocked to take part and learn dancing. Irish dancing has always been popular in Ireland and when the Irish came to Glasgow during the course of the hundreds of years, they probably brought with them their famous dancing art so it would be no fluke that a young girl from Drumchapel would eventually pick up on it at some point in their lives. The dance classes were very well organized and frequently filled. Helen showed great leadership and was loved by all the young dancers who turned up faithfully where they learned routines and fitness but mostly it was about young kids having fun. Some, to this day, still talk about those evening classes and with huge smiles on their faces.

The Youth Club at St Laurence's also provided the young males with boxing lessons complete with equipment and the stage in the hall was used as the ring. Mr Johnstone, en ex-boxer, took the classes and like Helen's dance classes, were a huge success. Mr Johnstone was a perfect trainer. He was experienced and taught kids confidence. He was a typical boxing trainer in the respect that he was hard but extremely fair. He was also a very nice man which helps when dealing with kids. He lived in Drumry Road and was a very popular and well-respected man in the community. The club also had many leaders and helpers who gave up valuable time to give kids in the area a place to congregate and take part in many activities.

In the grounds of the school quite next to the *Best Man Fall* wall there were two bushes. These proved to be a popular hide-out and recreational area where the kids would play a game of *Two Man Hunt*. Yes, in today's terms the title would be scorned upon as many girls took part in these games. It is not clearly why it was named *Two Man Hunt* because on several occasions only one would do the hunting. Basically it was a group of youngsters would run around the bush being chased by the hunter. The hunter would have to catch all to have the game ended. These bushes were home to many a wasp and bee family and the thorns were a hazard, to say the least. However, there was nothing dangerous in the eyes of those kids because they never looked at life as dangerous. It was anything and everything to get a laugh and to enjoy some fun.

The football pitch in the grounds was by far the most frequented part of the school after lessons. It was a small pitch in comparison to some other schools in the area. Many will recall Broadwood Primary's football pitch; that seemed like Hampden Park to young footballers but St Laurence's was fairly small but constantly full. The top end was the most popular because the fencing behind the goals acted as a net. Any bad shots over the net resulted in a visit to the back greens in Halgreen and sometimes in full view of some angry dwellers as their washing would often cushion the bad shot as it approached a Halgreen window.

The bottom end was only used if the top end was busy but no-one really fought for the top place. There was a mutual respect from the Inchfad and Fettercairn boys with the Kendoon people. It was a case of first come, first serve and all young players accepted their position. Boys would come from Abbotshall, Drumry Road and further up like Katewell.

Of course, not all the players were boys. From Kendoon there was a girl who played with the boys and she was actually better than most of them. Wilma Black was a gifted footballer and fierce competitor. She was by far the first female footballer many had seen or even heard of. Sure, some girls kicked a ball around the pavements but to be honest, Wilma was streets ahead and like we said, she was much better than a lot of boys. We have no idea if Wilma is still in the game or if she did pursue her interest further but what a player she was.

The advantage of the Inchfad boys was that they could see from their windows what was happening down at St Laurence. Especially if you lived from 62 up to 68 Inchfad. Their front windows faced the school pitch. It was only a few jumps down the stairs, run across the not-so-busy road and down the grass embankments to the pitch. The top goal was the be all and end all and the ultimate target.

The school also had fire escape which unfortunately attracted the curiosity of some youngsters who would run along the outskirts of the school windows supported only by the metal fence and the metal grid flooring that was extremely high up. These young ones ran dangerously without adult supervision as they would have had if there was a fire in the school but the kids were just curious and looking for adventure. There was a wall and a roof where the kids would dreepy from. Many a splinted shin and roaring ankle was had from dropping from a great height. It was all just a learning and discovery journey.

Near the pitch, towards Clydebank end, there was a makeshift mini pitch where young players played if the school pitch was full. A couple of young players went on to enjoy professional careers. We know John MacDonald, who went on to play for Glasgow Rangers, played on the pitch as a youngster in the school after hours but for sure, we know John Burke, who played for Dumbarton and Dundee United, played many a game on the mini pitch. In fact, he played there often with his buddies using makeshift goals and he would be there in all weathers.

The school pitch and the side mini makeshift pitch was most used during the 1974 World Cup. The games were live on TV during the months of June and July that year and sparked even more interest in the youths who hung around the school after hours. It was so popular that the grass behind the bottom goal was used more, the side mini pitch at the side towards Clydebank was extended and even the school Tarmac playground was used more due to the TV stations' live broadcasts. It was a marvellous spectacle...and the World Cup was good as well.

Fergie Russell, who lived in 68 Inchfad Drive, adopted the Germans as his team of the tournament, and they would go onto become eventual winners, as did the brothers Gerry, Mark, Thomas *(Tam)* and Barry Grant. They had relatives from Germany so it was fitting they would be supporting the host nation. Stevie Nicol, who, with a twist of life's fate, now lives in Germany, was a supporter of the cup holders, Brazil . Those were the sides the young players took on when Scotland were eliminated in the first round. It may have been a disappointment for the nation then but the youngsters from the pitch just carried on with their adopted countries. Games of *Hit & Run, Two-a-Side and One-in* were popular from the smaller groups but often full scale side-ups of 8v8 or even 12v12 would take place in the small pitch. It is no surprise many of the young players went onto enjoy the game at decent levels from good quality amateur levels, junior football, semi-pro and full pro levels. No coaching was necessary as all skills were honed and developed by watching the twenty-minute snaps of On The Ball and Football Focus plus the Match of the Day and Scotsport and Sportscene.

There was no such thing obviously as cable TV in those days where kids nowadays think they are spoiled but the kids back then watched and replicated what they saw plus added their own swing to things. Those were all self-creations in the end and made up for decent players who could hold their own.

Christmas morning was the most spectacular sight, clearly, at St Laurence's pitch. Freezing temperatures, often icy underfoot, were no deterrent for hungry young players who couldn't wait to hit the pitch and show off their new strips. We have no idea as to why but you can imagine today the kids can boast a range of replica shirts from the top English Premiership teams but in the early and late 70s the kids actually had the full kit and we can only imagine the Saturday night television broadcast of Match of the Day was the main influence. Having said that, the kids back then bought bubble gum packs associated with football cards and this is where the kids got to see the bright and broad range of colours. It is hard to think of a housing scheme in Glasgow like Drumchapel full of kids with Crystal Palace kit, Chelsea , Wolves, Leeds , West Ham and Spurs but that was the case. Fergie Russell had the Chelsea kit, the full kit, complete with the neat number 4 on the shorts. Stevie Nicol had the West Ham kit, Tam Grant had two kits in the one Christmas. Santa must have liked Tam. He had both the Wolves strip and the Leeds United kit. He even had the famous garter tie-ups with the number on them. His brothers also had full kits but Tam's was more known as he turned up on Christmas morning with one kit and then changed into his other kit. It was indescribable and a wonderful thing to see with such a young boy from the scheme. Cammy Johnstone, a brilliantly gifted technical player; dawned the Spurs outfit at an extremely early age. It is unclear where he got this strip or how he even came to ask for it but he was well-known in the area for his bright white tight-fitting shirt with the Spurs emblem, the dark blue shorts and the dazzling white socks. He was perfect for the Spurs strip.

That World Cup in 1974 was the catalyst for young boys. Perhaps it was the age and the timing of the World Cup but it was a perfect tourney.for the young boys growing up. Live games were magnificent, if you were lucky enough to have a coloured telly. The Russells were the very few people in the street to have a coloured telly and they got it well before the World Cup '74. One of the street dwellers recalls the time he had the pleasure of watching football in glorious colour…

'I remember watching the screen in awe. The first time I saw a coloured TV set was in Fergie Russell's house. Strangely enough, it wasn't a football game but Saturday night TV. My parents were going out with Fergie's parents at a night out in the Goodyear Social Club. May King was our babysitter for the night and I remember sitting there in my pyjamas watching The Dick Emery Show in full colour. It was mesmerizing. May flicked the channels and each channel seemed to get brighter and brighter. You have to understand, we didn't have a coloured TV set and I had never even seen anything in colour on

TV. Don't get me wrong, young readers might think we were poor but no-one was poor; we were all the same. No-one was rich either so we didn't have anything to compare to. Black & white TV sets were just the norm. The Dick Emery show was amazingly bright. Even the characters he played were bright and that is saying something considering one of his characters was decked out in the basic Harrington jacket, denims with the high turn-ups and the Dock Marts. When the football was on it was even more fascinating. There was one game in particular played at Wembley and I couldn't believe how green the grass was. This is why we named the side pitch (the makeshift one) at the side of St Laurence's 'Wembley'. The grass on the TV was much more spectacular than that of our own wee mini makeshift effort, but nevertheless, we named it Wembley to make us feel more important and to give us the feeling of being real players…just like that of the ones on show at Wembley – the real Wembley!'

St Laurence's in the background

St Laurence's Pitch
View from the Vernon's house

The Drum:
The Swimmies

As you got closer to the baths in Drumry Road you could not mistake the chlorine smell that oozed out of the building's ventilators. For any kid, the excitement increased as you neared the main entrance. Once inside you paid your fee to get in and the turnstile would click and you were in. Such a fascinating moment and the excitement would rise.

In the 1970s the baths were popular after school and at weekends with many youngsters flocking with their one towel rolling up their swimming costumes; neatly tucked under their arms and off they went.

When you were inside the baths you had to walk through the steamy changing rooms where a row of saloon-type doors would be swinging open and shut as kids, and of course adults, would come and go between the already swimmers to the new arrivals.

In those days you got stripped in the tight cubicles and jammed your clothing and belongings in hard-cases orange rectangular boxes. The time you had in the pool was determined by the sequence of coloured bands the attendants would hand you. You handed over your orange box with your stuff and in return whichever colour sequence was at the time; you were given a wrist band of that colour.

Your exit was determined by a siren that would ring inside the pool's complex and on the main wall beside the large clock was the different coloured lights. If the siren wailed and the white light was flashing and you had a white wrist band on you were out. No questions asked; your time was up.

As you handed in your box you made the short journey along the cubicles and you were met by a small foot pool where you were requested to steep your feet before entering the big pool. There were shower facilities as well where you could wash before you took the vital plunge into the big chlorine sea.

The swimming pool in Drumry Road was almost purpose-built with its arch roof, large windows at the main entrance and boasted a nicely-spaced cafeteria area for the after-swimming munchies. It was spotless and extremely well-run. It was also strict but you can see why as the deep-end was quite deep and the people responsible could not afford to let their guard down – literally speaking.

At the shallow end of the pool, the big windows were the gateway to the back-end of the baths that comprised of the bramble bushes and over and through the bushes you got a nice view of the tail-end of Beattie's biscuit factory and a rather large chunky site of the very famous Goodyear Tyre factory. The deep-end was the north-facing end where the big window divided the pool and the cafeteria and if you looked through the north-end of the pool's window and focused further through the cafeteria you could see Drumry Primary school and a bunch of busy traffic that came from Kinfauns Drive and the area from the Dalsetter end of The Drum.

The baths were a great place to go if you could swim. Each summer holidays the baths were full of kids and Saturday mornings were extremely popular throughout the year. One former regular to the baths tells us his account and the many memories he fondly has with his time at the baths…

'I remember the baths very well. I tried the springboard but mistimed the part where I was supposed to launch myself into the water and as a result got a nasty red stomach from vaulting belly-first into the pool. The diving dale was a no-go and I'd like to think it was reserved for the more experienced and braver of us all. I would often sit in the cafeteria with my famous caramel toffee lollipop that we bought for 2p and sit on the high chairs at the pool window and watch people dive off the dale, summersault from the springboard, and the highlight was when the swimmers would dive-bomb at the deep-end to create a huge splash at the cafeteria window. When you are ten-years-old there is nothing better than having wet hair, minging of chlorine, your hands are all shrivelled up and wrinkled from the water and you are sucking on a lollipop watching the bigger boys and girls making giant splashing actions against you as you sit at the window.'

Another former Drumchapel dweller and a regular to the baths in the 1970s was quick off the mark when she gave her recollection of her time at the baths. She said: 'It was just around the time Marine Boy was on our TV screens on a Saturday morning. Just watching that wee guy with his underwater antics made you want to go to the baths. As soon as he was off the screens me and my pal would grab our swimming costumes and wrap them and our brushes into a sausage roll-type knot in our towels, tuck them under our arms and off we went to another world. It was magic! We would spend ages in the pool; sometimes paying to get back in again once our band colours hollered us in and off we'd go again. We never crossed the 6ft line though as the attendants were very strict and you can understand now why they were strict but we were happy with the halfway line. You could tell the chancers from the real swimmers as the chancers would still be clinging to the rounded ceramic water channel that went round the whole perimeter of the pool and you could get a really good grip. We would grip our hands onto the rounded edge and kick our legs behind us creating what you would deem today as annoying splashes but we were young and having fun. The real swimmers would venture out into the middle of the pool showing their obvious swimming skills and capabilities. The attendants knew who were the chancers and who were the real swimmers because you could not kid them. If the attendants thought you were not up for the deeper-end task they were not slow in letting you know about it and would instruct you back to the shallow end.'

Back at the cafeteria…

They did a wonderful pea and vinegar in-a-cup that was a great seller and a brilliant pre-caramel toffee lollipop. Well, if you could afford it. Basically the cup was a polystyrene cup filled with green peas mashed up with vinegar. Perhaps anyone in the know would tell us better about what went into the cup but green soggy peas and vinegar is all we really know and it tasted marvellous. Whoever did the kitchen or even came up with the idea of peas and vinegar in a cup, designed more for tea or coffee, was someone who knew their way around a stove and had a clear vision of what after-swimmers needed. Anyhow, and no matter what, the cafeteria was a very filled place and not only splashers of the shallow and deep-ends but some folks would come in off the back of their shopping trip at the nearby shopping centre to enjoy the many drinks and treats on offer.

Let's go back to the early 70s where we detail a true story that happened in the Drumchapel swimming baths…

A full family consisting of a two-and-a-half-year-old child, his father, his uncles, and his grandfather, all attended the baths one Saturday morning. The young child was the first to get ready under the watchful eye and guidance of his father. The screaming noises and the splashing of the other kids in the pool was very exciting for the wee boy. He could not contain himself. He thought he belonged there, too.

Somehow the wee toddler found himself in the water by taking a daring plunge. Totally fearless.

An attendant was always quick off the mark but the grandfather had another idea. The wee boy was lifted out of the water then thrown back in again.

Much to the dismay of the attendants the grandfather was swift and acted in a manner he thought necessary. As the young child hit the water he disappeared under for a few seconds before popping up and immediately began to show instinctive swimming skills. Because of his grandfather's reactions that day the young boy became an accomplished swimmer and went onto enjoy many a great day out in the Drumchapel swimming baths. Had he not reacted in this way there is no doubt the wee boy would have gone on to have a fear of water and would not enjoy *The Swimmies* as part of his Drumchapel childhood.

The Swimmies were a magical place for the kids of Drumchapel to congregate. The aroma of chlorine would linger the air, competing for a nostril spot with Goodyear's rubber, and the inviting mouth-watering chocolate wiff from neighbouring Beattie's.

Diving, jumping in, ducking your mate's head underwater, and the effort of looking like you were a good swimmer to convince the attendants you were qualified enough for the deep-end all made for hunger pains. It built up quite an appetite. Some kids would take the short trip to the shopping centre afterwards where they would accumulate some sugary treats from the pick 'n' mix section of Woolies. In other words, they'd pilfer the swedgers.

Others were quite fortunate to have an uncle who worked at the baths and made sure of handing out some freebies: like the famous pie and beans.

The baths were just part of the childhoods enjoyed by thousands upon thousands of kids who had the great privilege of growing up in The Drum. Later on the baths would enjoy a revamp with a complete upgrade and makeover and as a result became categorized into the new-age terminology of a leisure centre but to the people from The Drum it will also hold a special place in their hearts and will almost likely be forever known as *The Swimmies.*

The Drum:
The Seven Hills

U nless you lived in the top part of Inchfad Drive you've probably never heard of the Seven Hills. The Seven Hills were situated in the rolling field towards Clydebank .

The name Seven Hills may have been tributed to either Fergie Russell, who lived in number 68 Inchfad Drive, or one of the Grants: Gerry, Mark, Thomas, Barry or Lynne. In fact, most likely someone else could lay claim to naming the Seven Hills but either way, it showed some creativity of which the kids growing up there had in abundance.

The Seven Hills were man-made sand humps and yes, there were seven of them. Actually, there were eight humps but one was soft and flattened and in the end it just crumbled and didn't qualify for the title. And anyway, Seven Hills sounded more like a spaghetti western and this is where the name came from. The kids in Inchfad used the hills to hide from the Indians. The imaginary Indians would attack the Inchfad cowboys from the far west – Clydebank – which seemed quite fitting as there was always rivalry between the industrial town and the sprawling housing scheme.

The Seven Hills were a great place to play. It was full of imagination and in part, played a role in the minds of those kids who would spend hours there carrying out *Cowboy* and *Indian* plays. Yes, the kids who hung around the Seven Hills even rode their imaginary horses. The sand there recreated the galloping dust affect as the Inchfad kids skipped and neighed their way across the great plain.

One of the former Inchfad gang recalls: 'The dust we kicked up as we pretended to be on horseback ended up in the turn-ups of our flared trousers. Remember, this was the 1970s. I guess it was not so much as a spaghetti western but more like a Bolognese bollocking because our parents would often have their sinks jammed due to the amount of sand when they did the weekly washing.'

The Seven Hills' experience also brought back memories for a former play-mate. Here he gives us his account of the secret gathering and self-proclaimed play area: 'The Seven Hills was a magical place to hang around. Most days, in fact every day, we only really played football down at St Laurence's pitch or the makeshift pitch adjacent to it that we called *Wembley*. The Seven Hills was where we played out our *Cowboys & Indians* roles and it was a brilliant place to escape. It was too far to hear our parents yell us in for our tea or worse: bed time. It was a journey for us to go there and yet it was only about 100-yards or so from our closes but the vast open space, the Kilpatrick Hills in the background, (those were real hills) and the distant sound of the flowing traffic on the dual carriageway that was the gateway to the North of Scotland; was a fitting place for a young kid growing up in the 1970s. It looked huge and the patchy grass that was saturated in sand made our secret play are a wonderful place to carry out all our film fantasies. In school we were introduced to Enid Blyton's Famous Five. Well, we had our very own gang: *The Magnificent Seven*…although there was about twelve of us…*Seven* just sounded film-like. Well, I mean, you had *Seven Brides for Seven Brothers,* and *The Magnificent Seven* and although technically we had eight hills in our plain; the number seven just sounded so right and in the end, for the sake of dispute, the eighth hill was just the leftovers from the other seven hills.'

Further down from the Seven Hills was a sand-pit. Once again, self-created by the kids from Inchfad. The hill was very steep and the drop, although not dangerous, was a great place to roll down. Some of the boys would take their toy cars to the sand-pit but fear of someone stealing them these boys would carry their toy cars in their pockets as they took part in the tumbling down the hill. Toy cars, model trucks and buses and even the occasional toy solder with the sharp pointed edges would be stuffed down the trousers of the boys as they raced others down the long hill from the sand-pit. The higher up you started and the faster you went resulted in the more dizzy you became.

One boy flashed his mind back to those sand-pit days when he said: 'There was more than one way to get a dizzy buzz back then but I remember going down the hill watching the world come at me at a great pace and ferocious angle. We didn't do drugs but if there was such a thing we created our own mind altering experience. As you rolled on your side you would see Clydebank to your right just roll around. It was a hoot to see their high-rise flats hang upside down for a second or two and if you were really gemmy you tumbled on your wilkies *(forward motion rolling beginning with the tucking of your head into your chest and a wee push and off you went)* you

131

would have a really amazing experience watching the likes of Paisley and Johnstone hit you in the face every second or so. The more dizzy we got the more we wanted more. The best hit was when an airplane would fly over The Drum, as it did every few moments, you would see planes upside down and at great speed, too. In all, it was a crazy but wonderful place and time to grow up. I am grateful we didn't have the technology we have today because I feel the kids today are missing out on so many things.'

The Drum:
The Clubs

The Scouts, The Cubs, The Boys' Brigade and The Life Boys were all close to each other. The Scout hall was home to The Scouts and The Cubs adjacent to St Laurence's Primary school. Across the grass football pitches at Halgreen from the Scout hall was where the 77th Boys' Brigade and The Life Boys took part in their Tuesday night's activities and routines.

One former member of the 77th B.B. recalls his adventures and with fond memories. He said: 'The 77th B.B. during my time was organized and run by the Brown brothers and other members like Irene *(nee Phillips)* Nicol. They were great leaders and held together a very well-run institute. The base was in Drumry Primary and was an extremely successful unit. The football team was very successful and many great young players who played for strong amateur sides on a Saturday and Sunday played on a Saturday morning for the 77th. There were many players and probably too many to mention but Mickey Williams stood out as one of the top players from the 77th. Most games were played in Victoria Park down at Scotstoun but I think that was mostly because other teams in the area played in our league and the parks at Victoria Park were quite large in numbers so there was always league games being played simultaneously.'

Another fellow member added: 'The 77th B.B. football team played in a number of kits; they were really well-looked after but the most popular kit we wore was the West Ham strip. I don't know why this was but the West Ham kit was our home kit for a number of years. We must have looked the part because we even had the numbers on the back and each Saturday you were guaranteed a freshly-washed and even ironed kit because the people who ran our club were very organized and took their roles as leaders very seriously.'

Another former member of the 77th said: 'The club was an amazing place to be involved in. The Brown brothers and their staff were always kitted out immaculately and they commanded a lot of respect because they were compact, honest, and knew how to organize things. I remember a great occasion when we were treated with a huge surprise at Christmas. It was a trip to a Christmas pantomime. The trip was tremendous. The bus took us all into Glasgow; we got out of the bus in a uniformed and deployed fashion as you would expect with such a well-run unit and we were given a night to remember. We were also given treat bags with sweeties in them for the journey there and back. Memories like these can never be erased and thanks to the great people who ran the 77th; I was one of the fortunate kids in Drumchapel to have taken part in a brilliant time of our lives and many friends back then are still friends to this day; and a large part of that must be in part due to the 77th Boys' Brigade.'

In May 1979, Jimmy Creswell started a boxing club that would go on to produce some outstanding young fighters. Ian McGirr, who currently coaches the boxers at the club, was an outstanding boxer and represented Scotland. Ian was also a Western District

Scottish and West Counties champion.

There were others who fought and represented the club and made a positive impression. The stewardship, coaching and dedication from Jimmy Creswell and his team resulted in a successful boxing club who unearthed and rolled out some great boxers from their conveyor belt of talent.

The club's birth began with dedication and drive and a thankful £1000 sports fund contribution.

Another superb indication of how The Drum was famous for producing greats and by the greats.

Charlie Kane and Graham Hughes were two other terrific boxers under the watchful eye of Jimmy Creswell.

Charlie's titles include: Scottish Featherweight, Lightweight and Welterweight champion. He represented Scotland at international level and Great Britain in the 1988 Olympic Games. Gold medal at L/Welterweight in New Zealand and several youth titles. An extremely impressive record.

Graham Hughes' record is also impressive with being twice Western District champion, Scottish finalist twice, Scottish schoolboy champion and British finalist, as well as Scottish youth titles.

Jimmy Harvey was another huge influence in the community of Drumchapel and his boxing club at the Argo Centre produced boxers of high distinction.

David Savage and Ronnie Carroll are well-known for their boxing talents and endeavours and have been praised and held in high regard by their peers and fellow professionals.

Young David Savage is highly tipped to go on to great things in the sport; he comes from a line of boxing history and with his clever and skilled style, he has given The Drum an added injection. The young boxers of Drumchapel can look to David jnr as a prime and shining example and hopefully one, some, or many, will work as hard to emulate him.

Ronnie Carroll's mark in the boxing world is another reason to be proud of our sports people from Drumchapel. Ronnie was a highly-talented boxer. He had a great mix of being a technical fighter but very, very tough all-round. His courage knew no bounds and he has gone toe-to-toe with the best of them in his weight. Ronnie's motivational skills are legendary. If he wasn't fighting he was talking and encouraging; and so many young boxers have learned from his European and world experience. A great asset to the world of boxing and a great asset to have in and around the area of The Drum.

Football clubs were ten-a-penny in Drumchapel. Many players went on to enjoy careers in the amateur, junior and professional leagues. A lot of teams formed around the scheme and on Saturday mornings and afternoons the dressing-rooms and pitches of Dalsetter were jammed with boys and youths from all over the scheme and beyond. Sundays, too, were filled with more clubs taking on other teams from Drumchapel and all over the city.

Spurs Boys' Club held their prize night at the Goodyear Social Club with special guest, Alex Ferguson. The date: 4th of July, 1975.

It was a surprise for the boys of the club but news soon filtered about the famous Scot's booking for the evening. That year Spurs were successful with the different age-groups winning their various leagues and cups. There were a lot of medals and trophies being handed out that night.

One of the young players learned of Alex Ferguson's proposed presence and informed his mother. The boys were asked to wear their best and many wore nice suit jackets and ties. This one particular player did not own a suit jacket. Out of the whole street where a few boys played for the club, this young player was all set to be jacket-less.

A neighbour's quick-thinking soon solved the problem. Two boys were sent to Kevin Peddie's house as it was known he owned a suit jacket. Kevin was older than the jacket-less boy and although not much taller, he was larger in jacket size. It was the only option available at such short notice.

The jacket didn't look that bad once the boy put on a pullover over his shirt and tie and under the jacket but the sleeves were far too long. The jacket was of good quality and as it was a loan there was no way any tailoring work was going to happen.

One neighbour suggested pinning the sleeves to make it look like the jacket fit the boy and it worked – until Alex Ferguson called the boy up for his medal.

The boy walked up proudly to applause. Alex Ferguson took the medal in one hand and shook the boy's hand with the other. The pinned up sleeve dropped and Alex Ferguson's hand went a quarter the way up the boy's sleeve.

It got a few laughs from the other boys and their families but a loud wise-crack came from one of the boys' fathers: 'That's it, wee man, yer first Masonic haun'shake.'

The Drum:
The Shows

The shows made annual trips to The Drum that stretched back decades and generations. Most people remember the shows beside the swimming baths and where the sports centre was later built. It was a unique piece of spare ground surrounded by wasteland and the famous brambles bushes. The Telecom buildings were to the East pointing towards the Dalsetter pitches end of the wasteland.

The annual visit from the travelling people was like a gift from above and brought magical colour to the scheme. It wasn't just little sideshows but the big wheel, the umbrellas, and the frightening dive bombers, were all on show. Some people refer to the shows as the carnival but you could say *showrnival* if you like; either way, it was a carnival erected by people who knew how to put on a show. For those who can remember way back, the shows were originally on the grounds of where the supermarkets Cooper's and Fine Fare would eventually be built. As those supermarkets were incorporated into the shopping centre the shows were relocated to the side wasteland at the side of the swimming baths. This was to be their best position and made the shows and the people who worked them more and more prominent.

Former dweller from up-the-hill remembers with great passion his encounter with the shows…

'I always remember hearing about the shows were

here and they were building their rides up and getting ready for some high energy entertainment. From my window at the time you couldn't see anything but the chimney smoke from Kendoon and Abbotshall but when the big wheel was starting to be formed you could see very faintly its big metal framework get higher and higher as the hours went by. On a clear day you could see the work unfold only by each metal attachment being bolted higher than the next but at night when they tested the lights it was pure heaven. The big wheel was the first sign that the shows were nearly ready to accept the flock of thrill-seekers.'

Another former resident who grew up up-the-hill recalls his time of excitement when he first got a glimpse of the dive bombers from his bedroom window…

'I was about 8-years-old when I first saw the shows from my window. I lived in the same street for a few years before but my first memory was when I was 8-years-old. I couldn't work out what the wee red peanut shape was or when it disappeared behind the tall tenement buildings the wee yellow one would pop up. It was fascinating to watch and I remember begging my parents to take me there. All I could think about was these wee coloured bullets and what made them circle the sky like that. I don't think anyone at that time had ever seen anything quite like it. When we got there the dive bombers were obviously much larger close up but I was terrified. It was unthinkable for me to be allowed on as I think there was an adult only situation with it; the ride was just not for kids. I remember the paintwork being shiny in some parts of the dive bombers and patchy on other parts. It was most likely down to wear and tear of the paint but the buckles from the safety fasteners made me realize even at that age that this wasn't vehicles from outer space as I had imagined in my room but indeed a real-life thrilling experience; because real people were inside screaming their heads off as the yellow end of the dive bombers came down in an almost head-to-ground fashion before making a swift turn and heading back upwards to the sky at the same time as the red end would follow it in swift motion. The two cars were at opposite ends of a large pole-like apparatus. Absolutely frightening and to this day I have never seen a ride more exciting or more thrilling.'

The shows were a dazzling prospective from parts of Drumchapel if you were within sight and the higher up you were in the scheme you got a great view of the big wheel and the dive bombers.

When you got closer to the shows, the crowds would swarm in a hurriedly but exciting fashion. The closer you got the more you could feel the heat from the engine running trucks that powered many of the electrics and generators. The cables would be tucked under giant rubber mats and when you finally entered inside; the surrounding wagons, the aroma of candy floss, and toffee apple, would hit you. The trucks roaring in the background to the popular music that was blasted out of the speakers at each ride helped to pump up the atmosphere and excitement. The dodgems were there as were many of the little sideshows where you could win a goldfish for fishing out three rubber ducks with an extended arm hook. Simple, but very effective and a lot of fun.

Some of the travelling people were highly-skilled at many things. One of them stands out and it would probably be unthinkable for a person not from the travelling community to achieve. That is, the brilliant gift of being able to stand up right in the middle of the waltzers; take your money off of you, spin you round as the ride revs up to a whirling frenzy; and when your whole world is going around your head – building up to a vomit excursion (especially for the girls) – the guy can still pick you out, hand over your change and ask you out for a date.

You spin a non-travelling person around like that and you will confuse their day-of-the-week, have them recite the alphabet backwards, and be able to do the moonwalk backwards on a horizontal airport escalator…facing in the opposite direction.

Travelling girl Katrina attended Drumry Primary but only briefly as her family would take down the big wheel and head off to somewhere else. I remember how good she was at counting. It was no surprise to see her at night exchanging money with adults as she handed them their change and with great speed and accuracy. We never really got to know how good she was at anything else in class but she sure knew her way around the money bag that was strapped to her.

The Drum:
Real Characters

Morris

When the TV programmes were coming to a midnight end the famous yell of, *'Mornin' Record!'*, would blast out across the streets and covering a great distance. Such was the depth of the voice, the man in mention was no other than Morris or Big Mo as many referred to him as.

Morris delivered the Daily Record late at night. It was, of course, the newspaper that had the next day's date on it as the paper was printed and dispatched throughout the country late at night. Any breaking news that happened after print would have to be heard on the radio or on TV because once that print run was complete there was no going back.

Morris collected his big bag of Daily Records and marched through the scheme late at night yelling every few closes his now very famous call, *'Mornin' Record!'* Members of the neighbourhood would scurry down in their slippers with coins in hand; hand over the bronze and silver and in return Big Mo would pull a paper from his loaded satchel and with one hand present you with a neatly folded paper that you could tuck under your arm and head back up the close. Big Morris was friendly and charming and extremely well-loved. When you talk about the famous names that came from The Drum you have to add Morris to that list. Everywhere you turned you either saw Morris or heard him or heard of him; such was his popularity.

For us, it wasn't the journalists that brought us the news stories but Morris himself. If it was an earthquake in a land we couldn't even pronounce or a shocking cup exit by a big club; it was Morris who broke the news to us. Anything that happened in the big wide world outside of the world of The Drum was brought to us by the big guy who would announce his news cry over the street-waves and the scheme was more the wiser of what was happening on the outside world.

Morris had many followers. Small groups of young men would escort Big Mo around the scheme in all weathers. No matter what, Morris and his entourage were there to bring you the latest.

He was also an avid Celtic supporter but that made no difference to the Rangers fans from the scheme as both sets of fans got on extremely well with Morris. He often joked and bantered with Rangers fans but all in great spirit. No-one had a bad word to say about the quiet yet loud-voiced unassuming gentle man.

Mr Gilbert

Mr Gilbert was a Church Minister at Drumry St Mary's in Drumry Road. Right next door to the baths the Church was a spiritual home and very often used as local community meeting place, youth club and just about anything that got the locals involved. Many a jumble sale event took place on holiday days and weekends.

Mr Gilbert was a hard-working Church member as well as Minister. He thought nothing of it to get his sleeves rolled up and attend to the bushes in the grounds of the Church. He would take his man-of-the-cloth collar off, change into a neatly-pressed open-neck shirt, and prim and trim the hedging and pick up any street litter that the wind brought in. It was a tidy and very well-looked after Church.

Mr Gilbert's door was always open and he was one of the fore-runners in that part of Drumchapel to have given young kids extra activity after school hours. He was also an avid football fan and loved nothing more than taking part in a kickabout with young up-and-coming stars from The Drum.

He ran a great little football hour-and-a-half up at Essenside Sports Centre. Back then the only time the young players got to strike the back of any net was if their team was lucky enough to play in an important game at Dalsetter, fortunate enough to play for their school team, or if they were even lucky enough to be part of a successful team that got to finals.

The indoor facility at Essenside was a breath of fresh air for the youngsters of Mr Gilbert's Church but others were more than welcome. Mr Gilbert was only interested in young members of the community having fun and getting a good honest organized game of indoor football. One ex-player recalls his time taking part in many of Mr Gilbert's football hours…

'I was not a member of Mr Gilbert's Church as such because my parents were not really the religious type so Mr Gilbert never really knew me except for maybe the fact that I attended Drumry Primary. A close friend of mine at the time used to play under Mr Gilbert's guidance and so I decided to take it upon myself to sneak my way in. I admit, I was expecting an ear-bashing or a definite no from Mr Gilbert because I never took part in his Church's activities. How wrong I was. Mr Gilbert was the most pleasant man you could ever meet. Here was me thinking I had no chance as an outsider in his footy sessions and yet he knew me and knew all my family. He taught Sunday school classes and many of my circle took part over many years. I was quite surprised but pleased that he knew my people because it meant I was well in there with his Essenside sessions. Wrong again! I had to wait my turn patiently like everyone else. No-one got any special favours because of who they were or who they weren't but the wait was well worth it...I was brought into action after 15-minutes and I never looked back. I guess today my love for five-a-side football stems back to my first-ever experience with Mr Gilbert up in Essenside. When I take part today and I strike the back of the net I always think back to my first shot on target under the watchful eye of Mr Gilbert.'

Like any elder in any community there has to be a level of discipline and Mr Gilbert was no exception. He was extremely fair but when we all boarded the bus excitedly to go to Essenside from Drumry Road we all had to queue and board in an orderly manner. Mr Gilbert was indeed a superb member of Drumchapel's community and many people will remember him fondly. He was, in a way, very much like the Reverend in the TV hit series *Little House on the Prairie*. Reverend Alden was the character and he was so like Mr Gilbert in so many ways. Ironically Mr Gilbert shared the same name as one of the main characters in the hit show. Wee Laura Ingall's real name is Melissa Gilbert. A twist of fate, coincidence or just astute observation…we will never know.

Ken the Barber

Ken came to Scotland from Poland. It is unclear how or why he came to Scotland but many say he fled his country to escape the war.

He was a quiet and an unassuming man. Many young men and elderly gentleman would flock to his barber shop in Drumry Road. Even young boys would queue and stand on the hairy floor for a regular clip and the popular short back, and sides.

Ken was just one of the many who brought an international flavour to Drumchapel. His short crop of white spiked hair and moustache made him a stick out. He was often on the brunt end of humour due to his accent but he was a fine gentleman who served the community and took a joke on the chin as well as giving back some classic lines.

A small boy turned up early at the barber's as Ken was opening up. The boy seemed to be in a hurry as his family were expecting relatives from down South. It was an unexpected and rush visit but the mother wanted some small errands for the guests and she also wanted to make an impression on them by turning her normally unkempt hooligan into a prize prince.

It was common for boys to take a note with them explaining to Ken what kind of style the boy should have. On this occasion the mother rushed the note that included the 'haircut' style, a messages list that was meant for the butchers and the bakers, and instructions for the boy on how to accomplish these tasks. She was so flustered about the guests coming she mixed everything together. Time was of the essence.

The note read:

Dear Ken,

- Please would you be so kind to oblige my son with a shortbread and sides?
- Please make it a thick cut and don't be dilly-dallying around talking to folk.
- Be as fast as you can.
- I want to see 6 slices. The last time it was only 4. Count them before you leave the shop.
- And don't be poking your fingers in.

Ken's English wasn't the greatest back then so you can imagine how confusing this note must have read to him.

He told the wee boy in broken English: 'Does your mother know I'm a barber?'

Mr McClements *(Jackie)*

One of the biggest and respected characters in Drumchapel was a gentleman by the name of Mr McClements. Hopefully the spelling is correct as he and his family thoroughly deserve their place in Drumchapel history.

With a bit more research and findings (we tried) we could have brought you more dates and facts. Mr McClements lived in 64 Inchfad Drive, with his wife Theresa *(spelling)* and two kids, Louise and John.

It was in the early to mid-seventies when families of Chilean refugees arrived and were spread around the Inchfad area. They could well have been all over the scheme but for factual records the street of Inchfad received the families from South America.

At the time Chile was under political pressure and so many fled and sadly, many were killed.

We are sure, up to some points, that Mr McClements had something to do with the success of integrating the Chilean families into the community. The kids had seen dark-skinned people as it was quite common but not with a Spanish language and accent. Two Chilean characters became prominent figures and are still talked about, even today.

Tulio was studying to be a dentist and one of the bedrooms was kitted out with his studies work. We were all allowed in to look and it looked like a scene from Star Trek. It was fascinating. Tulio spoke English but had trouble understanding the weans in the street. We were allowed to look at his books, sit at his big desk, look (but don't touch) his sharp instruments and we were definitely not allowed near the mercury.

There is no doubt in Mr McClement's influence. We have no record of what his connection was but even if he was just a supportive neighbour, he carried that duty out superbly.

He involved and encouraged the kids to mingle together.

The other Chilean character (*and we say character with affection*) was Mauritio. We always thought it was

Morrisio and asked him if he delivered the Daily Record in his native Chile. How naïve kids can be. We already had a Morris who did this and we thought all Morris' delivered papers at night.

Mauritio was an exceptional footballer and it didn't take long before the local teams wanted to snap him up. He taught some of the boys special tricks and flicks and on first glance they looked out of this world. We had never seen anything like this before.

The integration was a huge success. We would often play against the Chilean families at football. The smaller boys our age, the teenagers, and the fathers took part. Not once did we beat them at any side-up game. They were just too skilful.

The McClements were a clean-cut and well-groomed family. They looked it, too. They were a great family to have in the street and whatever role Mr McClements played, he taught us all tolerance, patience, and the importance of looking out for one another. With whatever connection he had with the refugees from Chile he did it quietly, firmly, and to a great success.

Just one of the great Drumchapel characters who graced their presence in a great community.

John Oliver

Today, John Oliver runs a chain of successful businesses in Drumchapel. He doesn't need any introduction to anyone who has ever lived or still lives in The Drum.

He is currently perhaps best known for his taxi business and his function suite but many of Drumchapel's residents remember him fondly when he started out.

He has come along way since those humble beginnings from his grocer's van to the Wee Shop on Inchfad Drive. The Wee Shop (as it was and may still be affectionately known as) is mentioned already in one of the chapters but stepping aside from John Oliver's business acumen and savvy; he is also a superb public figure and great ambassador for anyone, not only if you come from The Drum.

John has put a lot back into the community. He does it quietly and doesn't seek the publicity. A man of distinction, there are very few who have worked as hard to get where they are now and John Oliver is a perfect example of how to get your head down, sleeves rolled up, and work as hard and as long as you can to achieve things in life.

For the folks of Drumchapel, Mr John Oliver is the perfect role model and a much-celebrated figure in Drumchapel.

Walter Matuszczyk

Mr Matuszczyk, like Ken the Barber, came from Poland but we know more about Mr Matuszczyk than of Ken. His origins are more clear.

Walter, as he simply known as, lived in Drumry Road with his family: wife Jessie, and sons Anthony, Christopher and John. He does have family outwith The Drum.

Walter was a sharply-dressed man. He was rarely without his trademark shirt, tie and braces. He was a very well-recognized gentleman in the community and his homemade soup is legendary.

His football background is probably the reason two

of his sons, Anthony and Christopher, took the sport up. We will never know but his background in football may well have been an influence.

The weekends in the close of the Matuszczyks were filled with the aroma of Walter's homemade soup. There was nothing that ever tasted better. He made enough for his family and made sure the neighbours were never left out. Upstairs, Mrs Russell would send her son Fergus down to retrieve a big pot and it was enough for a whole family to get tucked into.

Walter was also an extremely funny gentleman as well. When he had a few drinks in him he would tell really great stories about his life growing up in Poland. They were heartbreaking and entertaining at the same time. All of which could easily be translated into film; they were that great.

Walter's legendary tale of how he came to Scotland is another classic still talked about today. On a wee night upstairs in Mr & Mrs Russell's house, it was Eleanor Nicol, who asked Walter: 'Why and how did you come to Scotland, Walter?'

Walter replied: 'We left due to the difficulties at the time in Poland. A friend of mine and I headed for the train station with our bags. We didn't speak much English but we knew some words. I just asked the ticket master, 'One return and one no come back again.' And here I am.'

Sadly, Walter passed away at a young age but he will forever be remembered as the perfect gentleman who gave the people of Drumchapel a taste of true classmanship in the art of humbleness, humour and dignity.

The Drum:
The Girl in the Cardigan

I went to school with a wee lassie, and halfway up to Cleddans Primary, I would meet another wee lassie.

Susan Steele and Suzanne Reading were in my class and we were close to each other. Partly because Susan lived a couple of closes away from me and it was with her and her dad that I began my school journey.

It kind of made it a lot easier to break into what I now call *eleven-and-a-half-years' enslavement of constitutionalised education that would eventually give us enough information that would allow us to work for large corporate entities; clocking on a Monday, battering ourselves into the grind before clocking off on a Friday; where we would eventually blow it all on letting loose. Then being skint enough that we would have to go back to the grind and do it all over again. Otherwise known as slavery.* But, that's for another story.

Suzanne was a nice wee girl – then she vanished. The teacher, Mrs Wilson, broke the news that our wee playmate was heading off to Australia. To us 5-year-olds we'd heard of Australia, as some friends had relatives who emigrated there, but it could have been at the back-end of Knightswood, as far as we were concerned.

In the playground we played and ate our pieces but there was something missing. It was Suzanne's skipping and singing that was missing. The corner where we played was just too quiet.

Susan was a quiet wee girl and I only knew her and

Suzanne. The school was nice with a nice teacher but there was something missing.

I never took to school and still to this day I hate Sundays. I guess the smell of Dettol and the creaky swinging doors through corridors with the blast of a teacher's vocal instruction, mixed with some silly wee rhyme, haunts me.

For me, Cleddans was a strange school. Looking out of my bedroom window everyone was heading down the way towards St Laurence and Drumry and I was heading up the way. I envied the others as they had bigger groups all heading to school and it was just Susan and I heading off on the upward trail to a lonely place. Well, I cannot speak for Susan but Cleddans was a long way up the hill for nothing.

I was in Cleddans for a very short time when I proudly told my parents that I could read. They obviously didn't believe me as I had only started school. They were in for quite a shock.

My mum went off into our bedroom and brought out a book that my sister owned. I sat on my mum's lap and began to read out the following:

'Onky upona timmy.'

Both my mum and dad looked at each other and asked me to read it again.

I read out loud: 'Onky upona timmy.'

It didn't take my dad a third reading to work out that I was reading words exactly how you would say them. I know that sounds kind of crazy but that was indeed the trick to it; you read a word exactly how it sounds to you.

I never discovered that on my own. It was the school that taught kids in a method that was designed for speed learning. It certainly worked.

What I was reading was the first part of *Goldilocks & the Three Bears*. It was *Once upon a time*.

We learned all about the alphabet and that process was in normal time for 5-year-olds but how can any adult explain the letter *C* is for *Cat* then expect that kid to be able to pronounce the *C* in the word On*ce*? You can't, it takes another course of education but the school scrapped this format and way of learning just about the time I left for another school. I must say it was extremely effective and might have been the reason I did well in English and have always had a love of words. I thank *Onky upon a timmy* for that.

My spell at Cleddans was short as my sister was about to start school and she opted for Drumry Primary. Her best friend Lynne Vernon were very close and we lived in the same close so it was always going to be inevitable that Karen (later Karyn) would go with Lynne to Drumry Primary. The distance was a bit longer but as we lived on the cusp of the border we could choose which school we wanted to go to.

I was asked if I wanted to change schools. Lynne's older sister Sandra was one of the guide-type of pupils who looked after the younger ones at Cleddans and she was one of my babysitters later on so it was quite a decision. I got on really well with Sandra and of course, throughout this book you will read my affection and respect for her and her whole family.

I chose Drumry. I knew a couple of boys who went

there so I changed schools. Cleddans was a fine school and I have great memories there but I eventually left Cleddans and reported for duty at Drumry Primary.

Suzanne Reading was gone...to Australia...and Susan Steele was hanging around her own wee pals; plus her sister Audrey, more. It was the end of my relationship with girls. Or so I thought.

My first day in Drumry was strange. For some reason the class looked bigger than me. I am sure that was down to my imagination bonded by the fact a wee daft boy from round my corner in Inchfad saying I should watch out as the Drumry boys are harder than the 'Cleddans poofs.' I didn't need to grow up and learn he was just a wee idiot and his name doesn't mean anything because he himself lasted about a month.

I was met at the door by a lady that scared me: the Head of Drumry Primary. My sister went in quite the thing with Lynne Vernon. Both skipped all the way in after the line. Nothing sells better than innocence. When I think of them both now it might have made a good *Little House on the Prairie* scene with Mary taking the hand of her wee sister Laura as they scuffled their shoes all the way into Miss Beadle's class. Of course, that scene would come some short time later as Little House wasn't known to us yet.

The lady at the door turned out to be a fine lady but it wasn't until later that I would be taught by a lady who is still one of my biggest influences to this day: Mrs Doran. I have no idea if she is still alive but she was by far the best teacher any young pupil could ask for. She didn't just teach – she encouraged.

The boys at the school played more football than the boys at Cleddans. I have no scientific back-up for this but that was just the way it was. John MacDonald and his friends were some of the best players in the area at the time and John MacDonald would go onto play with Glasgow Rangers. FIFA leader João Havelange said John was one of the best young players in world football. What a weight on anyone's shoulders that must have been.

The girls were more friendlier than those at Cleddans. I might be mistaken and I am sure there must have been nice girls at Cleddans but I only ever knew Suzanne and Susan. Sandra Vernon was different as she was a lot older and became my babysitter.

Drumry just seemed to have nicer and friendlier girls. Fiona Graham and Angelina Walker were the most vocal and even boys didn't mess with them. They weren't wee tough nuts or anything but they commanded a bit of respect. Angelina's big brother played for the school team with John MacDonald so that might have swayed in her favour and Fiona was a really nice girl who was not afraid of her own shadow.

I say these things with affection as both girls were extremely friendly, easy-going, and very funny.

There were other really nice girls in the school like Angie Graham, Joyce Miller and Alison Brown.

It was another girl I was closer to, though. I remember the teacher presenting me to the class – which was really embarrassing. In those days the desks were made up into twos. The object was to encourage boys and girls to learn together.

There were a couple of spaces available but my eyes

were fixed to a wee girl who sat on her own. She had a very friendly face, looked almost cheeky-like, but shy at the same time, and her cardigan draped over her tiny shoulders. As the teacher asked where I wanted to sit I pointed innocently over at this wee girl's desk and off I went. She didn't say much but I remember her smiling at me as I sat beside her. She moved over a little away from me to give me more space. Her manners were really good and she began to giggle. I remember having a similar experience with Suzanne Reading at Cleddans. I grew up with the thinking all girls giggle. Thanks to Suzanne and this wee girl in the cardigan I was proved wrong in my later on years.

We didn't learn anything except get to know each other. It was the first day back at school after a long summer break so neither the teacher or the kids were up for burying their heads in books.

When the playtime bell rang it was a bit of a relief. I knew a few boys from around Inchfad and near where my grandmother lived in Heathcot Ave and Drumry Road. I knew Anthony Matuszczyk and a few others like Angelina Walker. Angelina lived in Heathcot and my grandmother knew her family well so it was not as if I was starting all over again.

I got involved in a little game of football with a group of older boys who all chased a battered tennis ball around. None of the boys were any good but I made my first impression as a footballer when I trapped the ball, drew it back and lifted it like a pro. The girl in the cardigan was in the nearby shed half-playing and half-watching me. She smiled a lot at me but I thought she smiled at everyone and she probably did.

My first day in Drumry Primary flew in. It was a short day just to get all the kids back into it but we were all back home in the afternoon to get rid of our itchy trousers and stiff shirts. School uniforms are the most uncomfortable item of clothing you can wear. If you were lucky enough to have new shoes for school you knew all about it: they were murder.

My sister and Lynne Vernon skipped out of school together. I am sure they stopped skipping when they were in class but they skipped in and skipped out. Now when I think back, they must have been trying to wear out their shoes to get a new pair.

The boys and girls all raced out of the school and headed out of the two main gates. To the South, the Drumry Road and Heathcot kids headed for the lollipop lady, and the North gate was always jammed as the most populated. Kids from Abbotshall, Halgreen, Kendoon and Dunkenny; and adjacent streets to the hill: Kerry Place, Fettercairn and Inchfad.

I trickled out of the school with the girl in the cardigan in front of me; then she was behind me; then she was beside me. That cheeky wee smile was always there. I never knew where she lived until one day out of school, some time later.

I was playing a simple game of football within St Laurence Primary but strangely not on the pitch on the West side of the school but on a small stretch of grass to the East, at Kendoon Ave. The grass was just freshly-cut so this was exciting. It looked like Wembley. I can't recall how many of us were there but it was a bit full. Perhaps ten to fifteen all on this tiny long but very narrow piece of grass; that had skinny trees all staggered along this stretch of grass.

I saw the girl in the cardigan but she wasn't wearing her cardigan. She was in a red pullover. I recognised her instantly. She was with another girl playing in long grass but every now and again her head would pop up. Unknown to her I could see her. It gave me some idea as to who she was and where she lived but I knew I would see her the next day in school.

That next school day I was off. I had picked up an infection of sorts and was not in school for a few days. I enjoyed it. I watched all the kids going to school and I was off. My only worry was someone would steal my place next to the girl in the cardigan. I had to get better.

My illness turned out to be nothing but a small fever. As it happens a couple of other kids were off too with the same thing.

On my return to school the girl in the cardigan was not there. I thought she was moved to another class. I sat in my seat but there was no sign of the girl. It crossed my mind that she might have a sister or a brother who wanted to go to another school and she had to join them. I didn't really know what to think but the girl in the cardigan looked like she came into my life and disappeared.

I was paired with a guy I call Robert. For the life of me I cannot remember his real or second name but the class was not exactly fifty percent boys and fifty percent girls. Some were paired and some were not. Robert was loud and very annoying. The girl in the cardigan was a lot quieter and a lot easier to sit beside. This guy was a talker and the girl in the cardigan was more of a thinker and a smiler.

For the next few days I had to sit beside Robert, the annoyer. I am sure he might have been a decent wee boy out of school but he was the first kid I had ever seen or heard that was cheeky to a teacher.

My playtime was spent just playing football. I was allowed to play on the small pitch with the older boys but not yet ready for the big pitch. That space was reserved for the superstar players. Football was everything to me. I loved when the bell rang for playtime but I hated it when the bell rang to come back in again.

To my surprise the girl in the cardigan finally reappeared. I believe she was off school for a good few days and our teacher put us back together again. She was still the girl in the cardigan but she had a different cardigan on. This time it was a near pink cardigan and not her grey one.

She was popular, well-liked, and very well-accepted. Everybody liked her. She was just one of those wee kids who was very likeable.

I knew her name, obviously; then I found out exactly where she lived and what close, as we would walk home together. I stopped thinking of her as the girl in the cardigan because the weather was becoming a bit chilly and everyone was now wearing thicker pullovers and jackets.

The girl in the cardigan now became the girl in the anorak.

The girl in the something became my best friend at school. We would often laugh at the silliest of things and she would watch me play football. I felt really proud because by now I was accepted onto the big pitch where I would enjoy a game of football with the older guys. The girls kept themselves to themselves with their elastic ropes and chasing each other around the playground.

The girl, formerly known as *the girl in the cardigan,* invited me to her house at lunchtime. It was an honour because no girl had ever invited me or asked me to anything. I felt special. I felt a sense of pride and of course I accepted.

Her house was not that far away from our school. It was a few chases, a couple of hop-scotches, and we were in the close. My fondest memories were meeting her dad for the first time. I cannot tell you how scared I was as she told me he was a boxer. I was expecting a bruiser of a man to be waiting on me but instead he was a fine gentleman and could not do enough for me. He also gave me something to remember that I could not leave out of anything childhood-related.

We sat in the kitchen and he made us tomato soup. I remember how hot it was and it took ages to cool down. He gave me and the girl in the cardigan a slice of Mother's Pride bread and told us to 'get stuck in.'

The girl in the cardigan started to tear small pieces of the bread and drop them in her soup. I'd seen this before but in our house it was considered bad table manners and if my mum knew I was a guest in someone's house and acting like I was feeding the birds she'd have gone nuts. The girl's dad sensed this and gave me reassurance that when I was in his house I was safe and was allowed to do things as long as they were under his watch and as long as we behaved. I ripped the bread and threw it in the soup and took the spoon and felt the warmth and the aroma of bread all around my face. It was just magical.

He was a really top bloke who was kind and generous. There was a hint of discipline about him but as I came from a good disciplined family I connected but I suppose when you have boxing experience you have to have discipline.

The first time I was in the girl in the cardigan's house was a great experience for me and I often think about it. Her dad treated me well; made sure we were in good hands, and he made sure we were allowed to be kids but most of all he made sure we were safe. I took to him instantly. He made a very positive imprint on my young mind and to this day I warm when I think of him.

The girl in the cardigan and I continued to be the best of friends. She never annoyed me, she never disappointed, me and she was always there. If she wasn't sitting next to me in class she was watching me play football, offering me sweeties from her hand and just being a brilliant wee pal.

During a summer school holiday my family were accepted for a house in a new estate just outside Hamilton. It was part of an overspill plan that many say was to connect East Kilbride to this little village. It was called Little Earnock and this would be our destination just a couple of days before the school term was to begin.

I never got to say goodbye to the girl in the cardigan. When we left school at the end of term we ourselves didn't even know for certain if we were to be accepted. It was all just too quick. We packed up and left.

It wasn't until years later I found out the little girl in the cardigan was devastated when I left. I also found out she would write letters to me in the hope someone would find me but I never received any letters from the little girl in the cardigan. We just drifted apart and made a little piece of our history. Film companies could have made fortunes out of our story.

I thought about her all the time. I met new people in my new school but I always thought about the little cardigan girl. In hindsight it was all-too-stupid of me because I knew where she lived but she didn't know where I lived. The onus was on me.

I would later move to East Kilbride and just after my 16th birthday I received this letter through the post addressed to me. The only envelopes addressed to me were birthday and Christmas cards but in this particular month I received quite a few. It was exam time and my school sent me the dreaded brown envelope to tell me how much of a failure I was. National Insurance and the Youth Opportunity Scheme were bombarding me with nonsense I didn't want to know about and lots of other trash mail you get when you move from school kid to adult. I threw most of the letters in the bin. Any envelope that is not birthday blue or non-official white goes right in the bin. Even today I hate official-ism.

One particular day I collected the mail and amongst all the government briefs was a small handwritten envelope that was a welcome site. It was neatly-written with a very impressive scroll style to it. I had no idea who it was from but it definitely got my attention. I opened it without a hint or a thought of who it might be sending me a letter.

It was from the girl in the cardigan. I have no idea how she traced my address but you have to applaud her for her work. It was as impressive as it was amazing.

To this very day we are still very good friends. She was there for me when we were very small kids and she is still there for me, as I am for her, and her support has been a great drive for me. I hate to call her the girl in the cardigan but that was how I met her and it stuck. The funny thing is she has no idea that was how I named her. I didn't want to upset her and I know she would argue it was not a cardigan but a jumper. There are just some things you have to keep to yourself.

The famous girl in the cardigan could well be a book on its own.

Her real identity is Margaret Savage. Former pupil of Drumry Primary and Kingsridge Secondary. Many know her as Maggie Savage and nowadays simply Mags but for me, she will always be Margaret in public and for me personally: *the girl in the cardigan.*

The Drum:
A Week in the Life of...

Monday:

School, work, and a new beginning to the week. Nobody likes Mondays: The kids would head off to their schools with faces tripping them. They'd scuffle their shoes along as if to delay their entrance through those dreaded gates. Nobody likes Mondays and nobody likes school anyway, but school on a Monday is a lethal combination.

'Mind yer dinner money!' the mothers would yell as the kids clutched the 60p in their pockets like it was the crown jewels. Back in the mid-seventies 60p covered a whole week's dinner money that had to be handed in on a Monday morning. The 60p these days would not cover the gerkhins on a burger but back then it stretched from Monday to Friday and it got you mince and tatties, pies in all their forms, and the favourite of them all: pink custard and caramel cake…*yum.*

Nothing happens on a Monday except for some evening youth clubs and entertainment. Some boys would be lucky to have football training that evening but most clubs trained Tuesdays or Thursdays.

The teachers tended to use Monday for some interaction and to get to know the kids more. A lot of the kids would write or draw how their weekends were and it did make for easing the Monday blues.

In Drumry Primary Mrs Doran was famous for her Monday routines. She made it very easy on the kids and she had this wonderful ability to make our

Mondays feel like they were Fridays. As strict as she was in her teaching methods (and she had to be) she always included fun in her lessons and Monday mornings were just brilliant when the crayons came out and the large blank sheets of paper. It didn't matter if you could draw; we all explained our weekends perfectly because Mrs Doran was a teacher who allowed and encouraged children to express...and it worked.

Tuesday:

The B.B., Girl Guides, Youth Club and the telly is no bad. At the 77th B.B. in Drumry Primary we were given our match schedule for the following Saturday morning's game. The 77th B.B. were famous for having a very good football team. Team captain Mickey Williams was just one of the accomplished and known players in the team, as explained in an earlier chapter. His task was to make sure we were organized and go as many games without a defeat.

The walk across Halgreen in the dark during the winter nights were great; as we discussed the forthcoming match but Saturday seemed a lifetime away. Four days until a game of organized football with strips, a lined pitch, and nets, just seemed too far away. It was four sleeps. Strangely we preferred to play away from home as Drumry's pitch was much smaller in comparison to our favoured Victoria Park.

Many of the football clubs had training on this night so the evenings for the kids of The Drum were full of activity.

Wednesday:

Midweek means mixed bag. Most of the entertainment was made up of games in the streets or some of our favourite TV shows happened midweek; especially Sportsnight. Now there was a TV show that we often thought defined class if any show did. We were only interested in the football but they sure as hell kept us hanging on as late as they could with showjumping. Not many people from Drumchapel were into showjumping. That was for snobs, according to us, but they did prolong that event until the midweek cup clash or the European Cup games.

Those Wednesday nights were just brilliant – for those kids who were allowed to stay up late. Showjumping stretched and stretched and cut away some of our extra stay up late time and to this day I detest showjumping. It is also a cruel sport, in my eyes, because horses are not made for jumping heights like that. They don't have flexible backs and the weight they push on their small ankles makes for a barbaric event, if you ask me. Some might agree or disagree but in any case it pushed back what we felt was more important and that was the fitba. Sod showjumping.

Thursday:

Youth clubs flourished on a Thursday. I can't remember exactly if the St Laurence Youth Club was on a Tuesday or a Thursday but Tuesdays were pretty much the same as Thursdays so we'll call it Thursday for argument's sake.

Helen Rankin's famous Irish Dancing nights were

testimony to all that was great about kids growing up in The Drum. Helen was the main focal point in the street of Inchfad Drive but she was also well-known and loved in other areas because girls from all over the scheme used to flood her dance class each session.

Mr Johnston's boxing club was popular. The stage in the main hall was used as the ring and although the equipment was not exactly state-of-the-art, as you would find today, it was enough for a great session; but the experience and knowledge from Mr Johnston made the club a success. He was a well-respected coach/trainer and clearly knew his stuff.

Friday:

By far the best day and night of the week. Home early from school and allowed to stay up later than normal. The feeling that there was no school the next day was special. I don't think any kid liked school. It wasn't cruel to the teachers but there were other more important things to be getting on with like: hide-and-seek, fitba on the school pitch, one-man-hunt, kick-the-can and jumping dykes.

Fridays were also renowned for the insurance man and the many financial district administrators – also known as debt collectors. The insurance men were funny people. Mostly bespectacled gentlemen and they had all their collective data on all the households in tattered books held together with elastic bands. They were nice people and often left homes with a fully belly full of tea and some Jammy Dodgers. Friday was pay day for a lot of working folks back then and as you can imagine, most took advantage of no work the next day and having a couple of quid in their pockets.

The Vernon's and Littlewood's Pools agents were all welcome but the debt collectors mostly only saw the long dark hall and at the end; the back-end of a closed living-room door. I have no idea why but that was just their luck that not many people were at home at the time of their visits. What was it the folks back then used to say? 'Ye cannae take knickers aff a poor arse.'

Fridays were also for confessing – if you were of Roman Catholic persuasion.

Saturday:

Full-on parties. The greatest evenings were Saturday evenings. Everything just felt right about a Saturday night. Adults enjoyed their drinking sessions and the kids enjoyed extra pocket money from happy adults and the television was a dream. The whole of the scheme seemed to come alive. Many had previously taken part in the biggest past-time: football. You either played for your club in the afternoon *(and sometimes your school in the morning then your afternoon club match)* and/or you were lucky enough to go to see one or the other giant Glasgow teams, namely Celtic and Rangers.

Social clubs and halls were buzzing with events and bashes. The Goodyear was the main headliner but was then matched by the Golden Garter.

Sunday:

The places of worship were normally a full house on

Sunday mornings. Bells would ring around the scheme as neatly-dressed citizens of The Drum would congregate the many places of prayer. Sundays were also a day for visiting, homemade soup, *The Adventures of Black Beauty,* and silverside and sprouts.

It was also bath day for many of the kids. Bath, bed early, lights oot and school the next day. The most disliked part of the week.

The Russell Family

Karen Nicol (left) and Lynne Vernon

The Drum:
A Year in The Life of...

January:

It's New Year in the '70s. The 1st of January is always a hard day for every youngster growing up. Parents still in bed, hung-over, after finally getting to bed at 7am. The smell of cherry cake, waff of nut air and a putrid sickly stale beer, still-in-a-glass, fills the living-room. It's so strong it almost flips the festive cards that hang from one side of the wall to the other; both sides supported by blue-tac: adult plasticine.

We had visitors coming over at noon so the place had to be nearly re-decorated; well, just a tidy-up but it looks that bad we'd be as well giving it a once-over. There's an almost depressing feel in the air at this time. It's still dark; the New Year was brought in by a bevy of vocals and silliness; almost all-too-innocent. The days when getting drunk and dancing with your auntie were simple times of blushing amusement. There's many a wee Glaswegian child who gathered all their funny material just by observing the goings-on from behind a '70s swirly decorated couch.

There's nothing happening at this time and when I look out the window it's still icy; cold with a few tinsel flickerings of Christmas past at each apartment window. Music can still be heard but slightly dimmed across the neighbourhood as tenement residents sleep under coats and crumple on heaps on tiny sofas.

It wasn't long before my mum got the Hoover out and started whacking the corners of the skirting with her Electrolux. This is the day when a lot of people really enjoy getting bevvied as it is the last real holiday day; after the 1st it's all uphill from there; back to work and a big effort headlong into Easter.

It's sad for me as I am way too young to participate in getting smashed and the countdown back to school had begun. That new toy smell was beginning to disappear so we really have to give this last day the biggest whirl. Fortunately for my mum the visitors were late but for me I couldn't wait to get that party started and sparkled into full swing from a distance in my pyjamas. It's the time when I could get any biscuit I wanted; once your parents have hit that falling down and talking crap juice that kitchen cupboard is fair game and very much open season.

The 1st of January is not for your average Christmas turntable tracks but more of a reflecting mood like traditional Scottish thingamajig reels and yeehahs! The best stuff was when the 45s were tossed to one side and the real artists took to the floor…all eight square feet of it.

The worst month of the year, at any time, and for anyone. The ghost of Christmas past seemed like a million years away and already we are looking forward to the next one but it's ages away!

Snow caps clung onto the tiled tenement roofs just clinging on like grim frozen fingered death. The sun never really came out at the best of times so the whites of the snow had no reflection 'cept for two shades of pale.

School! Christ, I forgot about school. We go back next week. My Mouldmaster ball still smells of new rubber and with only a few scratches from yesterday's kerby game with the lassies, I now have to get my school uniform out…*yuck!* I hate school.

Mrs Doran will be asking us all what we got for Christmas and it will just bring back memories. I miss Christmas already.

Nothing happens in January. It is a dead month. It is dark but that pre-Christmas dark where all the trees at the windows glitter and give us the feeling Christmas is just around the corner. The Christmas trees are all gone apart from a few faded ones that might seem to have their lights on but there isn't any life at the window – everybody must be depressed. Reality has just sunk in and it's only the first bloody week!

I think they should scrap January and go straight to February. February is not a great month but at least the smell of Christmas has gone and it gives us a sense of moving forward. January is just a stuck month that doesn't tell us much or go anywhere. It's like a time trap but you can't shift into any gear.

It's only the 7th of January but already I'm thinking this is going to be a very, very long month.

New Year's resolutions are a waste of time. I just refuse to listen to them. They go in one YEAR and out the other.

<u>Here's my tips:</u>

Start your New Year's resolution in October. That way you will already have a three months' head start and you have plenty of time to drop out or change your plans.

When Big Ben strikes at 12.00 on Hogmany, refrain from promises, hope and unreachable ambition. Just utter the words, 'Well, that's 365 days I'm never getting back.'

Don't put off until January what you can easily start in September.

If you do have a New Year's resolution, keep it to yourself. Don't tell anyone what it is. This works great if you are still overweight the following year because nobody will be able to judge you.

February:

Snow seems to like February for some reason. The 25th of December is always raining or just frosty but not a real frost where you can slide; it is a damp frost like milk half-poured over a sugary serial.

February, however, *aha!* Now this is real snow. This is the snow I like to call sledge snow and snowman snow. None of your slushy buses snow where the thawed snow creeps up all the way to the top deck window of a 20 bus. This is the real stuff. Lots of people getting snowed in, pipes burst at the school, teachers can't get to school because they always seem to live in exotic places like Renfrew or the Southside.

Februaries do have their draw-backs, though. The inside of our bedroom windows are frozen. You can barely scrape your initials and it's freezing!

March:

Yaaaas!!! Easter is approaching. March is the month where most people lock themselves out of their houses for some reason. It's a funny month. I think people are just too excited at the hint of a wee bit of sunshine. We are now officially in the cardigan season. It is much too cold to wear a T-shirt but too warm for a Parka or a heavy pullover.

April:

Everybody seems to have their birthday in this month. It is mine but I thought I was the only one born in April. It turns out most of my family and a lot of neighbours. One even shares the same birthday as me. Mrs McClements from 64 Inchfad shares the same birthday as me, can you believe that? I think she's older though.

Easter is here. At long last. We've only waited four months to have something to celebrate. Easter is just like a cheap knocked-off version of Christmas because we only get one wee present in an Easter egg but it's better than nothing.

The lead up to Easter is funny. We get to bring boiled eggs into class with us and the teachers give us strands of coloured wool to slap on the egg for hair and we use ink markers to draw a stupid face on the egg. In some ways I kind of feel sorry for the egg because eggs do get a hard time of it.

We lock them up in wee boxes without air holes. We then put them in a cold fridge to suffer the cold then we take them out and boil the poor wee things. If that's not cruel enough we take them out of the boiling water, hold them against their will in a funny shaped cup and slice the top of their heads off.

Some eggs are lucky though as the slicing can be swift and final but some people just have no respect: they batter them over the head first with the back of a spoon then peel their shells off then cut them up into wee pieces before smothering them in a buttered outsider.

May:

The mornings are lighter and the summer school holidays are just around the corner. May has that *don't care* feel to it as we will be off school and back in what seems like a lifetime away – August!

The council come around and start to cut the grass. The end of May has that real summer feel and smell to it. Our street goes nuts when they cut the grass. All of us kids gather up all the loose cuttings and pile them high to make grass-like snowmen…except it's grass. I suppose we are actually doing the council a favour by scooping up the scraps of grass their giant cutters leave behind. Even the poor kids who suffer from hay fever manage to squeeze a few minutes into diving through the giant stacks of grass; before wheezing and scratching their eyes all the way home. I bet they wish grass-cutting season was in winter so they could get days off school. I wonder what the pollen count is then. Ah, yes, it only happens during summer season. I've heard a few people say that. Oh, well, what a shame. Hay fever sufferers suffer at the best time possible to be a kid – summer holidays!

June:

This is when it is still too early for sunburn but not dark enough at night to play hide-and-seek or kick-the-can. It is right in the middle of indecision time. Should we take a pullover to the swing park or even a cagoule?

June is putting green time at the park near the shopping centre. The warm mornings are great for running down to the park and grabbing the early spots at the wee hut on the green. The place is usually mobbed by lunchtime – especially if there is a major on the television; which runs through July, mainly, but we always get a wee taster during the sport channel.

For the older kids you tried your luck at tennis at this time of year. All the would-be Jimmy Connors and Chrissy Everts would be gathering at the tennis courts. Most of us kids would chalk a court on the roads where we lived and off we went with our tennis rackets, balls, imaginary net and the wee self-important ones who failed miserably in school and would go on to fail in life, would be the umpire.

July:

July, the warmest month of the year at times and you know when you are on holiday when July comes. Some families fled to sunspots like Blackpool, Morecambe, Bournemouth and our very own holiday destinations quite near us. Time to break oot the empty Fairy Liquid bottles for *skooshing* purposes.

August:

A mixed month. We knew school was coming close due to the back-to-school adverts and the shop windows changed from summer toys to grey and blue stiff-coloured shirts and new shoes. The new shoes were everyone's rage, if they could be afforded. A new pair of shoes took away the pain of having to go back to school. Even if the new shoes ripped the flesh off of your heels you still put up with the pain and anguish because no amount of torture beat the first day back at school.

September:

September is one of those *nothing* months. It has no real purpose except the nights look like getting darker and the temperatures closing down a few degrees. Septembers are like Tuesdays. The previous months are but a distant memory and all we have to look forward to is the October week and Halloween.

October:

The cold is starting to bite in, especially at night. The dark is closing but the school days are getting more exciting because we have the three main events coming up: Halloween, Guy Fawkes, and we've even been talking about Christmas.

It's Halloween time soon and already the shops are selling the traditional monkey nuts and witches hats.

November:

A worn-out tyre hangs aimlessly around a street pole, behind a dark frosty backdrop, and the smell of Guy Fawkes hits the back of the throat. Roll on Christmas.

December:

For many, December is the best month of the year. This is obviously down to the Christmas aspects but also it is a great holiday time as parties would flow throughout the Christmas and into the last day of December. It is a time where families get together from afar and take part in many ceremonies – like, getting drunk!

The Drum:
The People's Accounts

When my family moved from the town to Drumchapel it was like a new world for us. There was so much space to play and it was spotless.

Most families back then came from single-ends and overcrowded areas so The Drum was a very welcoming part of our lives.

As I grew up in Drumchapel I thought the whole world lived like us. I was not aware of other places as I was very young but the trip into Glasgow city centre on the bus was like going on holiday.

I have nothing but the fondest of memories of my time in what I call the best place ever to have a childhood.

~ Billy McQ ~

Drumchapel has changed since my time there but when I see an old photo on the internet it takes me right back to 1970.

That was the year we moved to The Drum.

I disliked school but I suppose most kids could say the same.

My life was the swing park near the shops and the Hecla Arms pub, I think it was called.

My dad drank in there on a Saturday afternoon whilst my mum and my aunt went to the shops. My sister and I would play for hours before being picked up by my parents and aunt.

We were never in any trouble as the swing park was full of kids the same age and it was like a drop off point to give the parents peace to shop, have a couple of pints and put a line on at the bookies.

When I think of the swing park I remember the spider's web and the roundabout. There was the normal way to rotate both and there was the sick way. Not sure if we meant clockwise or anti-clockwise but either way it was so much fun.

~ Carol Davidson ~

My memories are many.

At school I had the privilege of being House Captain of Gordon House at Waverley and had a wonderful time there.

My main thanks would go to Willliam Smith, Captain of 142nd BB attached to Drumchapel Methodist Church.

Friday was Company Night, Saturday morning was football; Sunday was bible class and mid-week, arts and crafts class.

Later I progressed to Essenside Youth Club. Great discipline there mainly due to fearsome but well-respected Mr Shorthouse, who was the sort of Janitor.

So many people then, facilitated our entertainments, probably not appreciated until now.

Also, I met my wife , who was from Drumchapel, but we only got together on The Isle of Man on holiday.

My best man was Raymond Gillespie. His dad was manager of the furniture department in Arnotts, I think.

My mum worked at Drumchapel Sick Children's Hospital and my dad worked in the Shipyards.

A great place to be brought up in the 60s.

Essenside Youth Club was opened around 1966/7.

Mr Shorthouse was always on the door and no admission without your membership card. No exceptions for admission without your card.

It was run by committee of paid staff and youth club members.

Activities included 5-a-side football, netball, badminton, table tennis, trampoline and a well-run cafeteria – again with input from the members.

It was very well-attended. Average numbers attending football would be around thirty and we had to patiently wait for the girls' netball to finish; although it was quite a pleasant sight to watch the girls.

Phil Bonnyman was a regular at Essenside Youth Club. He was a a very good all-round sportsman who excelled at football and went on to play for Glasgow Ranger's first team.

~ Colin Craig ~

I was Rangers daft but my whole close was full of Celtic fans.

Can you imagine the stick I had to take?

Especially as it was during the time of Celtic's famous *Nine-in-a-row* era.

I got my own back the night we won the Cup Winners' Cup in 1972.

Right after the game I went down to the ice-cream van and cleared its shelves. I bought Irn Bru for everybody up the close and hundreds of sweeties for the weans.

It was a silly act of celebration as I was actually steamboats and unknown to my wife I had actually acquired all of the goodies on tick.

It wasn't until the following week when the guy at

the van took about half my wage packet off of me.

That was just one of the great memories growing up in Drumchapel.

I can honestly say we never had any trouble at all. A lot of families were of mixed religion anyway and mostly all the closes had a mix of both Celtic and Rangers people and as far as I am aware we actually made it work.

We had the banter and some heated encounters but those were just through passion; we were never in any danger and never likely to cause any either.

Yes, Drumchapel was for me the best place as an example of how to live side by side with each other.

~ David Smith ~

Magic place, The Drum.

Lived there all my days until I got married and moved down South.

I attended Kingsridge Secondary school early 70s and I have very fond memories of life outside school. I hated it but the people, the neighbours and all my mates were the best thing about growing up in the big scheme.

My holidays were spent doon the coast during the Glesga fortnight fair.

Great times had by all but returning to play games of football on the streets and in the school pitches of Broadholm and St Pius were my treats of the holiday break.

~ Davie the Joiner ~

The Drum for me is famous for many things but I do have very vivid memories of Morris the paper delivery guy who would walk the streets of

Drumchapel each night selling the Daily Record to the people. I can still hear him cry out: *'Mornin' Record! Mornin' Record!'*

I also remember the football players like Gregor Stevens and wee John MacDonald. They were really nice guys as well as good players. I didn't know them that well on a personal basis and they probably didn't know me but they were always very friendly and would never walk by you in the street.

I watched both boys hone their skills on the Abbotshall pitches and for their wee teams when they were youths.

~ Hugh McD ~

First Love.

In 1954 Gene Kelly starred in a movie called 'Brigadoon' where two American tourists stumble across a mysterious Scottish village that appears for only one day every hundred years. Tommy, Gene Kelly, falls in love with Fiona and must choose between modern day America and the old ways of Brigadoon.

My experience of first love also happened in a magical time and place that was full of colour, innocence, and freedom.

The scene was set, purely by chance, two years before I was born. One day my father read an article in a newspaper about housing bosses taking bribes for houses.

At the time he was living in the Townhead area of Glasgow with my mother and three sisters. The flat, a single-end, had no toilet, no kitchen and only one room. The environment was filthy by today's standards and people struggled to get by on a day to day basis.

He was so angry he wrote a letter to the housing department that night. The following week he was offered a house in Lillyburn Place, Drumchapel.

The house was located in a quiet cul-de-sac, was in perfect condition, and had two bedrooms, a bathroom and a kitchen. The back windows looked onto a sea of green fields, a giant water tower and a farm. My mother was over the moon and they moved in just before Christmas, 1963.

Things went from grim to great overnight; as a family they had never lived in a house with its own bathroom, kitchen and room space. They soon settled into their new community and made lots of friends. In those days no one locked their doors and the word community really meant something. Most had come through hard times and all of the neighbours went out of their way to help one another.

The sixties kept giving and giving, jobs were plentiful and tons of new opportunities and experiences opened up to all.

People began to take holidays abroad, buy cars and tour further afield. Churches got in on the act by opening up social halls and organising mystery bus runs all over Scotland.

Young people expressed themselves with music and fashion. Flower power sprung its roots with bright colours, dance, long hair styles, music, festivals, 'groovy' new words and much more. The Beatles, the Rolling Stones and many others churned out thousands of vinyl records in a battle to be number one.

For the first time every home had electricity.

Cookers, fridges, washing machines, carpets, record

players and radios became must have items in every home.

Previously unvoiced masses were grabbing the headlines as good triumphed over evil; the Civil Rights movement in America was gaining momentum, laying seeds for future change and 400,000 people gathered to take part in a 'hippy' music festival at Woodstock farm, America.

It was as if we were coming out of a deep depression and the planet was wearing a smile.

My father didn't know it but the second half of the decade was about to deliver even more. At 6.50pm on the 10th January, 1965 he was blessed by the arrival of a son.

After work, he travelled to Redlands hospital in the West End of Glasgow to be with his wife and new baby.

Meanwhile, back at the ranch, my sisters waited with baited breath to get their first glimpse of their new baby brother.

Said enthusiasm soon wore off and was replaced by constant complaining and complete indifference. Cries of, 'Do I have to watch him', or 'It's not my turn', were commonplace.

One sister took me out for a walk with her friend in my pram and forgot to bring me home. At the tender age of four months, she had left me outside Mills newsagent. Luckily I was still there when she returned.

Another sister let go of my pram on a hill and it was only by sheer chance a bus didn't hit me as my pram whizzed across a busy road.

When I was old enough to walk things got better. Each morning I would wake up before everyone else and would sneak into my mother's bed. She knew I was coming, as mothers do, and would just pull up the blankets without opening her eyes. In her arms I was warm, secure and loved and she gave me the nickname 'Snookums'; brilliant!

On reflection she let me away with murder. If she thought I needed sorted out, she would delegate the task to sister number two, Kathleen the tomboy.

On the whole the girls were alright, although they did favour sister number three, Evelyn, and spoiled her accordingly.

As it turns out there were two other girls in our close who were the same age as me.

Life was simple and I didn't have a care in the world; every day was play day. Caroline Craig, Maria Houston and I played from early morning to night.

The seasons were in tune with nature and the summers arrived bang on time.

On our many adventures we would jump, fish and fall in the nearby burn which had a haunted tree hanging over it called 'The Hairy Mary'. There were many horror stories surrounding this tree so we avoided it at all costs.

We spent many hours chasing each other through the rolling fields that seemed to go on forever.

There was sand-pit in the vicinity that attracted children from other places, and the older boys made sure that they didn't step out of line.

Cows came right into our backyard and my mother, who was not Indian, told me it was a sin to hit them.

The farmer kept horses in a special field and you were not allowed to play with them in case they bit or kicked you. Sometimes they wandered up to a wall and you could feed them. They sensed fear so you had to relax in their presence and let them do as they pleased. On one such occasion I watched in awe as a big stud horse pissed in the breeze with his dangling fury in full view.

Sister number one, Marie, would track me down when it was time to come in. Embarrassed, she would chase me all over the street while the other children shouted and cheered. When tomboy sister number two, Kathleen, turned up, I would give up.

On Thursday 25 May 1967, my father's favourite football team, Celtic F.C., won the European Cup. They were the first British club to lift the trophy and all the players hailed from in and around Glasgow. Ripples of this famous victory spread far and wide and it is still talked about today.

Next, televisions and telephones arrived in our homes. The world was becoming a smaller place and it seemed anything was possible. The next logical thing to do it seemed was to visit the moon. And so on July 20, 1969 Americans Neil Armstrong and Buzz Aldrin took one small step for mankind. Needless to say this was watched by millions who gathered around TVs all over the world.

I'm still not sure why man visited the moon. Personally, I would have saved all that time, money and energy for a rainy day, or focused on a cure for cancer. That's the problem with good times, after a while people think they will last forever and always want more.

Just as change had entered my family's life overnight, the same would happen to me.

The writing was on the wall when I was sent to nursery school; being locked up from 9am to 3pm didn't sit well with my emancipated disposition.

Then when I thought things couldn't get any worse, they sent me to a place called 'school' wearing a uniform and a balaclava. I had no idea I would have to go to this place everyday for the next twelve years or so.

School was no place for a guy like me.

On my first day I punched a boy's nose when the teacher was out of the classroom and there was blood everywhere. The teacher returned to find me cleaning up the crime scene with the sleeve of my blazer. She went mental.

Everything was falling apart.

The family decided to move to a bigger house far away from all of my friends and my countryside paradise.

The clock struck 12.01am, December 31 st 1969 and the sixties were over.

We moved to a three bedroom flat in Drumry Rd, Drumchapel close to the border of Clydebank. Situated on a busy main road, I had no friends and no where to play.

Two years later I would come face to face with the unexpected death of my mother. I was only seven years of age and longed for my mothers warm embrace and times gone by.

The only thing I could do was pray and stay away from my father who had turned to heavy drinking to dull his pain. In those days there was no real help for anyone suffering a bereavement. My mother's death left a great hole in our family. It was a terrifying setting for any kid; to be literally left alone in the dark for long periods of time.

Given all the facts, I now realise why my father went to pieces. Today, the girls are all doing well and have produced their own 'new age' families with all that entails.

I have wandered down a million dead-end streets in search for those simple, carefree days that in reality will never return.

Nothing had come close to that magical decade, then, as Gene Kelly did, I found a way to travel in time and place.

All I have to do is close my eyes and listen to music and I am immediately transported to the place I heard it first.

Simples!

Also, the family culture and feelings of love I have encountered in Northern Spain have given me hope for the future and a brand new Nirvana that I can assure you will be full of colour, music and dance.

My paradise in Lillyburn Place, Drumchapel no longer exists; lost in time, but forever in my heart.

~ James McGinley ~

I was brought up in The Drum.

I left Kinning Park in1954.

It was a great place, like living in the country.

No tenements, a bathroom in the house, and open countryside. Great stuff.

We lived in 31 Kendoon Ave.

Drumchapel was still being built. We played out all day long. I remember *The Butty* being built; what a pub that was!

Ayton sandwich biscuits from Beattie's, Goodyear smell of rubber, and the Cutty Sark whisky factory.

I remember we used to wrap ourselves inside a lorry tyre and roll down the hill; it was great.

The Buck was going then; all mods gang.

In the early days a van came round with all we needed shopping-wise. The ice-cream man was called Tommy Ray, he sold screwtaps of McKewan's on a Sunday at a highly-inflated price.

I also remember the shopping centre opening. That made a great difference as people had to catch a bus to Clydebank to shop or go to a pub.

Happy days they were.

Served my time and moved in 1972.

Some of my friends: Andy McKellar, Stevie McGrath. Willie Harkins, Matt Wiseman, John Reiley, Willie Fitzpatrick, Davie Ferguson, and some other great people – bless them all.

~ **Jim O'Neill** ~

Oh, where do I begin? Started at St Sixtus' and although I have no recollection of my first year there I do remember my First Communion. I have never looked so good – until I got married. Two dresses but two very different sizes.

~ **Anne McC** ~

What can I say about The Drum?

I grew up there in the 1970s and we had the best neighbours, the best friends, and the best things to do.

It was the best grounding any wee Glasgow child could ask for.

I cannot thank all my neighbours and friends enough for making my childhood one to remember for the rest of my life.

~ **Jamie T** ~

I was a young 16-year-old; kicking about the streets

at Peel Glen.

I stayed in Summerhill Road from the age of 14.

Myself and a group of friends bumped into some street workers who were trying to get the young ones off the street and join their youth centre, which was based in a close at Kinfauns Drive called *Drumchapel Detached Youth Work.*

At first we just went for a laugh and any free outings but then one day the chance came up for us all to go away with an expedition called *Raleigh International.* Only myself and friends Kenny and Gizmo applied for it.

We had to get camping equipment together as we were off to Mugdock Park for the weekend with fifty other people from other communities; and after a long hard survival weekend you were getting told if you had passed the survival course; then going onto a week's survival course in London. Thereafter the chance to pick a country to go to from either Malaysia, Chile or Zimbabwe.

My friend Gizmo never even turned up for the weekend. It was just me and Kenny walking through swamps blindfolded at 3am. It was all mad but it was to see if you would survive these things in another country.

Kenny also left on the Saturday night. I was gutted and told the workers I wanted to go home but they talked me round with one more day to go.

Anyway, I stayed and found out on the Sunday I had been picked to go to London for the week and from there, passed my week's survival course and got told I was going to experience the expedition with *Raleigh International* in Zimbabwe for three months.

The Drum crew, and all of the detached youth workers, held a leaving party for me in the Kinfauns Centre before I left for three months.

I was 17 and going to Africa for three months. It was the best experience of my life and still to this day cannot thank my youth workers in Drumchapel enough.

I also remember when we got to Harare there were one-hundred people there from all over the world from: Scottish people to English, Welsh, Chinese, American and Australian.

I remember the first four weeks being very homesick because everyone was receiving letters from family and I wasn't.

After six weeks I got my first letter, from my *then* boyfriend, telling me my mum had just had her breast removed. She had found two lumps whilst I was away. I was so upset and was determined to go home but the workers there were great and got me to a phone to get in touch with my mum.

If it wasn't for her wise words and tone telling me that I used to stand at my bedroom window every day saying, 'it's boring, wish I had something to do,' and here I was in Africa doing something amazing and yet moaning to come home because of what had happened to mum.

I knew life was too short and I opened my heart and eyes to what a beautiful thing that was happening for me.

I even taught some of the kids English or *Scottish* in their school.

I also visited a malnutrition hospital which broke my heart but made me eat my dinners more and not waste so much when I got home.

I was also very friendly with an American girl, she was delightful, with a big heart. I even named my daughter after her.

I hope this story catches The Drum people as it's straight from my heart and head full of memories.

You can leave The Drum but The Drum never leaves you.

~ Kathleen Hill ~

My family lived through a couple of decades in Drumchapel. We all went to different schools at different times but we all shared the same love for our scheme.

When I hear about kids moaning that they have nothing to do they would do well to go back in time to my days.

We had everything you could ever dream of. We had imagination and played games I swear were invented on the spot.

Skipping the dykes, ropes, playing tennis balls against the close wall and the very dangerous clangers (I think they were called). They were two hard balls that knocked against each other to make a sound. It was bliss.

I've been away now for many years but my heart will always belong to The Drum.

~ Lynne Stewart ~

I have a soundtrack of music that I can relate to my time in The Drum.

I moved with my parents to Drumchapel in the mid-sixties and the songs on the radio then I have on records and CDs today and when I hear a certain song now it takes me back. The Dave Clark Five and

195

The Beatles always remind me of our move to Drumchapel.

I recall T-Rex and of course all us girls loved the Bay City Rollers. I can still smell our kitchen when my mum cooked when I hear Bye Bye Baby. Isn't it funny how these little things in life never leave you?

We moved away when I was in my late teens but living in Drumchapel gave me a solid foundation that has helped me no end in my life today.

I don't suffer fools gladly and I have a great knack of winning historical pop quizzes.

Thank you, Drumchapel.

~ Margaret Delaney ~

I'm an ex-Drummy boy and my greatest memories were the school day trips to the Bluebell Woods and the wee bus runs to the Art Galleries.

When the bus turned around the roundabout at Drumry Road and headed towards the toon it was another world for us weans fae The Drum.

We would all scurry for a place at the front of the bus upstairs to enjoy our big world view.

Great Western Road was a really fascinating place because it was the highway to the toon and the open door to a whole new experience for us.

Occasionally we would give the staff at the Art Galleries a wee bit of banter but it was all fun and nothing too cheeky. You wouldn't get away with being a wee brat anyway as our teachers were very strict.

~ Pat Smith ~

The Drum is famous for its famous people connections like Billy Connolly, James McAvoy and all the footballers but in the community there were a lot of people just as important.

I am not a religious person but I did enjoy a good Sunday morning cuppa and piece of cake in St Laurence's Chapel. I skipped mass and lied to my mum that I was there but a lot of us did. We only went for the grub and a chat and someone there would tell us who was serving mass that morning; which was handy because that was the first question our parents asked us on our return home.

The people in the Chapel were just the most marvellous people you could ever wish to meet. I was a teenager back then and you don't really appreciate your elders until you become one yourself. I cannot remember the names of the ladies there but one lady I do. She was Mrs O'Neill *(spelling?)* and I believe she went into politics later on. I am not sure if she was one of the ladies who served the tea but she was always around helping people and attending to everyone's needs. It is probably no surprise if it is indeed the same lady who took up a position in the political platform.

She was a remarkable member of Drumchapel and so were all the other people at St Laurence's.

I never did get the chance to say thank you until now. I hope my addition to The Drum book is accepted as I really would love to say my sincere thanks and to all the people of Drumchapel.

~ **Patricia McQueen** ~

I can remember the first time I saw Barney Platts-Mills.

I was walking down Inchfad Dr when this burgundy Jaguar pulled up outside number 90.

It was the same car as the one in Inspector Morse.

This big tall guy got out with John Lennon glasses on.

I said: 'Alright, big man? Are you lost?'

'No,' he replied.

I stay top flat at number 90.

It turns out Barney was a film director from England.

As the weeks went by we all got to know Barney.

We were always hanging around him and eventually he asked me and my best mate, Brian Gourlay, 'Do you guys want to be in a film?'

'Are you mad? Of course we do.'

The other guys in the film included: Derek McGuire, Danny Melrose, and Harpo Hamilton.

My parents had to go to my school with Barney to ask for permission to stay off school as the film was being shot in Lochgilphead, in Argyll.

We stayed in a castle owned by Caroline Younger, the heiress to Younger's Tartan Special. What a place! All this private land with tennis courts. The castle even had a dungeon.

The film was a Gaelic film called *Hero*.

Brian and I were fish boys. Our part started from this witch who takes two fish from this river and throws them on the grass. Brian and I turn from fish to humans – very believable.

While we were up there we learned to build a dry stone dyke and thatch. We built houses for the sets. Just being there watching how this film was being made; to a 15-year-old boy from Inchfad was just incredible.

I heard music on a Walkman for the first time there, listening to *Bat out of Hell*.

We were paid ten pounds a day. We thought we were millionaires.

I look back at my time up in Argyll; it was the best time of my life up there as a 15-year-old boy from Inchfad. A film star! It doesn't get any better than this, I thought at the time.

We went to the Edinburgh Film Festival for its showing and the film itself was filmed for Film Four.

The heroes from Inchfad: never forgotten.

~ Robert Hendry ~

* *Hero* was also an official entry for the Venice Film Festival.

I was a bit of a lad growing up in The Drum, hence the reason for my name change, but one thing I never did was back-chat any adults.

I was a daft wee boy but in The Drum our adults were highly-respected. They looked out for us and I can never forget that.

I am utterly convinced if I had been brought up anywhere else I would not have sorted myself out.

It was my Drumchapel surroundings that eventually brought me to my senses.

In other words, a lot of people kicked my arse and when I think back now I realize how right they were.

Nobody escapes a good ear-clipping when you are fae The Drum. If you think you are above your station there are many around you who are capable of bringing you back down to earth again.

Thanks, The Drum

~ Ronnie McT ~

Francie and Josie turned up at the supermarket in the sixties to open Radio Rentals, or was it Redifusion?

Francie in a pink red suit and Josie in a turquoise suit. Trousers at half-mast and brothel creepers on their feet.

Remember, this is before colour telly so seeing them in glorious techno blur was a treat.

There must have been about five-hundred weans all there to see them.

As they left on the back of a open-back Land Rover all the weans chased them as far as we could before they sped off into the horizon.

I also recall how the houses were allocated in Drumry Road.

Two bins in the middle of the road full off keys.

One with keys for two apartments and one with keys for three apartments.

The people were told to take their pick and swapping keys was okay; so folk could swap to be near their pals, et cetera.

~ Stewart Nicol ~

Growing up in Drumchapel during the 1970s was about the best experience I can remember and everything I learned in my early days shaped me up perfectly for the life I live now. I don't believe I would have achieved half of the happiness in my life had I been brought up somewhere else. Nowhere compares to The Drum and although it has been a long time since I last visited the dear old place I have great memories.

I was not too fond of school, as probably we all weren't, but life outside of school was terrific. The open space we had back then is a luxury in today's world. For a sprawling housing scheme we had a great swing park near the shopping centre, pitch-and-putt, bowling green and can you imagine this…tennis courts. We must have felt like snobs being able to boast about tennis courts right in the middle of our scheme.

I had many great friends growing up and from my nursery days to this very day I still have the friends I had back then. Such was the place and such were the people. We will never see its likes again.

~ Colin C ~

Ah! The Drum, what a place. When I think back and when I hear a record from former times on the radio that was out when I stoated about the streets in Drumchapel I can almost smell the biscuits from Beattie's biscuit factory and the constant noise of the double decker buses as they transported many of our residents into and back from up the toon.

My best memory comes in the shape of playing football for my school team in the Saturday morning then playing for my youth team that afternoon. Dalsetter was where we spent most of our time playing organized football and I still shiver to think of those harsh winters when our wee fingers were too numb with the cold to untie our boot laces. I remember some wee boys would be crying due to the cold. Some cracking players came from Drumchapel, mind you, and I am sure they will have many mentions in the book but we all remember John MacDonald, who went onto play for his boyhood heroes, Rangers.

It was a great time to grow up but you could grow up in Drumchapel in almost any decade before and after my time and the people would probably say the same.

~ **Derek 1963-1979** ~

I have vivid memories of my childhood but nothing as strong as when I was a kid growing up in The Drum. It might sound stupid to today's young people but we were very rarely in the house. We never needed much persuasion to go outside as it was a big open world outside of our bedrooms. The boys all seemed to play lots of football and the girls would be skipping rope, chalking out the close entrance for a game of peaver, or bouncing balls off the close walls. Some of the neighbours went off their nut; especially when it was raining as our rubber balls soaked in the rain and when you bounced the ball off the close walls it left wee circles all over.

The close I lived in was painted in two-tone with a dark wine colour at the bottom half and a cream colour at the top half. It was the cream half that showed up the evidence and sometimes us wee lassies were on the receiving end of a severe ear-bashing; especially if the close had just been cleaned.

When the boys and girls played together it was mainly so that we could thrash them at kerby. The boys used to cheat as they kicked the ball along the Tarmac so they couldn't possibly miss the kerb but we were better as we were netball players or just that we had more practise. I am sure the boys will disagree but of course, it was all in great fun and I shall cherish those memories forever.

~ **S. Davies** ~

Me and my wee pals used to make up wee lines of entertainment for ourselves. In the summer we stood on the dykes at the back and pretended we were the *Bay City Rollers* and in the winter we would hold wee pretend tea parties in the close as the rain lashed past us. We didn't have a care in the world. There was no such thing as boredom. All of us had at least a doll each and the lucky ones had a pram to go with it.

We all shared things anyway so it didn't really matter who had what and who didn't have what. Some people talk about being poor growing up but we were never poor. No-one had much in terms of wealth but we were rich in imagination and rich in other ways. No, we were not poor, we were just wee weans who grew up in a housing scheme and our parents worked, if they had jobs, in factories, were trades people or did anything they could to get by. It was the way it was back then but if I could do it all again I certainly would.

  ~ **Margaret D** ~

It's strange. When I think of Drumchapel I immediately think back to the school summer holidays. They seemed to stretch for ages and yet it was only a matter of a few weeks. Maybe it's just us looking back and missing our childhood that makes us think this way but I believe we had a better time growing up than some kids today.

The last day of school was when we were invited to bring in a board game or something to entertain us. I think the teachers didn't want to work either on the last day so we both had it easy but the wait for that last bell to ring was a long wait. When the bell did ring we all scampered through the gates, over the fences and even through the wee holes in the fences and off we ran yelling our freedom. We felt brave on that last day and we felt we could do and say what we wanted because six, seven, or eight weeks was a lifetime and the teachers would never remember a thing…or so we believed.

That high on the last day was quickly reversed by the low on the first day back. I would imagine all kids went through the same ritual when going back to school: early bath, uniformed ironed, and if you were lucky you had new shoes to wear. Probably all in the name of taking our minds off that we had to go back to school.

Back to school days always makes me smile now as I don't need to go to school but when I see the little ones going to school for the first time I always think of two things: my own time when I started school and the great line that goes like this…

A wee 5-year-old boy starts school for the first time. His mum waited patiently at the gates to collect him from his big day. As the bell rang the wee boy scurried out to meet his mum.

His mum said, 'Well, what did you learn today then?'

The wee boy replied, 'Not a lot, mum. I have to go back tomorrow again.'

That joke still makes me laugh. It must be ancient now, like me.

~ Mrs MacKay ~

The Drum:
The Weans' Stories

The ice-cream van and the lucky weans:

This story was mentioned on Radio Clyde and it is already in a book, but its popularity and being very Drum-related, we could not possibly leave out this classic.

In the 1970s Billy's ice-cream van used to come around a couple of times in the evening. Billy was as punctual as Big Ben but his sweeties tasted better.

The van made its way from Fettercairn all the way around the back of Inchfad and to the front of the street facing St Laurence's Primary school.

As Billy burlied his vehicle of scrumptious goodies, belting out the Roadrunner theme tune, all the kids raced not to the van but to the front gardens of each close where they stretched their necks upwards and yelled, *'Maaaaaaaw!* Gonnae geez 10p fir the van?'

At the bottom left-hand side of number 68 Inchfad, Mrs Russell was in her rollers and vanity got the better of her. She was desperate to get her daily pack of cigarettes but she couldn't face the van in her dressed state. She summoned a wee four-year-old girl to the bottom floor window where she dropped a crispy pound note in her hand and whispered, 'Get me 20 Embassy Regal and if they don't huv Regal, just get anything.' Meaning, another brand of cigarettes.

Well the poor wee lassie was at the van for what seemed like an eternity but she soon emerged out of the crowd carrying a cardboard box and struggling to balance it as she made her way one step at a time up the stairs of the close to Mrs Russell's front window.

The cardboard box contained a few cones, MB bars, sweetie necklaces, flumps, flying saucers, sherbet, strands of liquorice…and a bottle of skoosh.

The van didn't have Embassy Regal and the wee lassie did exactly what Mrs Russell told her to do in the event of that situation arising and that was 'just get anything.'

It was a Friday and approaching tea-time. Mrs Russell's husband, Willie was due home from his work and would have had a fit had he found out a full pound note was splashed out on sweeties at the van. A pound was a lot of money back then.

Quick-thinking Mrs Russell invited as many weans from the street as possible to get rid of the evidence. Even Scotland Yard would struggle to find any trace of DNA left as everything was gone in seconds. Even the cardboard box went missing, never to be seen again.

Wee Cathy's spelling dilemma:

Wee Cathy got into trouble for questioning the teacher.

She innocently asked the teacher how to spell a particular word.

The teacher gave her a tip when she said: 'Catherine, if you don't know how to spell a word, just look it up in the dictionary.'

Wee Cathy replied: 'But, Miss! If I don't know how tae spell it, how can I possibly look it up in a dictionary?'

Wee Carol's Enid Blighty's Infamous Five:

Our worlds were very much just like other kids growing up in any other part of Britain until our teachers introduced us to *Peter & Jane* books.

What an eye-opener that turned out to be.

Here was our little world full of tenement rows and busy streets with team loads of young people all mingling and socializing as if it was the last day on earth; then we met brother and sister, *Peter & Jane.* Thanks to Ladybird books we had something else to envy and to look up to.

They were the perfect family. They had a house that had up-and-down stairs, back-and-front door and a nice family dog. They got up to things we could only dream of.

The educational aspects were clear enough in hindsight but when the teachers walked up-and-down the aisles in our class-rooms; dropping off a *Peter & Jane* book at each occupied desk, it changed our way of dreaming about what we wanted.

Peter & Jane were more suited to the rich south of England by their appearance and their activities alone were enough to suggest they were definitely not like us. They were just so much better than us and even in illustrated pictures they were more attractive looking and handsome than us. It just wasn't fair.

If big Peter and wee Janey implanted a reality check in us wee Drum weans it was devastating to be introduced to another young team that literally blew some of us away: Enid Blyton's *Famous Five.*

How a crowd of weans could scour their village late at night with a torch, solving crimes. If any of us were out late at that time we'd be seen as up tae nae good and if we had a torch in our possession it would have meant someone in our group knocked it off to be able to afford the batteries and be accused of going on the rob.

The difference in those other children to us was breathtaking. Yeah, of course, those were only stories and illustrations but they were full-colour and made us look like mere charcoal sketches, in comparison.

Wee Carol was not impressed, or maybe she was just terribly envious of the fresh-faced coloured imprints of another so-called class of children?

'Haw, Miss! That book is pure pish. Nae weans live like that. It's aw made up, init? Ur they oan hoaliday or summit? coz that hoose looks like a hotel. I bet ye they ur the same as us…pure skint.'

'No, Carol, these children have been created for adventure. It is for entertainment and education. There are children who do live in houses like *Peter & Jane*'s and there are children who do take part in their own little adventures like the *Famous Five*. You can, too. You can all do the same as *Peter & Jane* and the five adventure children.'

'Nae chance, Miss. The weans in Enid Blyton's stories solve mysteries. Ye cannae dae that in The Drum.'

'Why not, Carol?'

'Coz ye'd be seen as a grass.'

'Well, why don't you and your friends search for something else? It doesn't have to involve crime.'

'Don't get me wrang, Miss, we dae huv adventures tae find 'hings.'

'Well, that's just great, that's a start. What kind of

things do you search for, Carol?'

'Burd's nests, Miss.'

'But, Carol, that is not nice. You can't go disturbing bird's nests and their habitat. You don't touch any eggs, do you?'

'Naw, Miss. The big boayz ur usually there furst and they swipe aw the eggs. The boayz are taller than us anyway and usually get tae the eggs easier than us.'

'Oh! Carol, that is shocking.'

'I know, Miss. It's murder bein' this wee.'

The teacher, clearly a nature and animal lover, or just a nice environmental person, could not answer wee Carol. The wean was right, *Enid Blyton's Famous Five* and *Peter & Jane* were just worlds apart…and the weans knew that. They accepted it and made up enough of their own wee adventures to suit their environment…and it worked!

The weans' new haircut:

Just days before Christmas Santa would come to the primary schools in The Drum, to hand out small gifts.

The gift may have been a toy car, a book, or just anything to put a smile on the faces of the kids. In fairness the schools were not shy in splashing out for the best they could give the children of Drumchapel. It was good for moral when a kid was treated well.

One on the girls received a toy plastic hairdressing kit. There was nothing dangerous as all the little instruments were made of plastic and rubber.

However, after about an hour playing 'pretend

hairdresser' she whipped out real scissors from the kitchen drawer and proceeded to give her brothers and their wee pals a real haircut.

Yes, you can but just imagine, the state of those wee boys and their hair. They were only allowed to parade themselves in the streets for a very short time before they were all escorted down to Ken the barber in Drumry Road for a tidy up.

At one point Ken, who was Polish and must have thought Scottish weans were mental, refused to cut hair that had already been cut by another barber (he said, with tongue in cheek). It wasn't until he was given a good wee bung, when he finally owned up that he knew who the other barber might have been, did he finally square the boys' hair up.

Thanks to Ken, the boys all received nice wee short backs but thanks to the wee lassie – *nae sides!*

The Drum:
Time Machine

You've been robbed at mouse-point Oh, how the world has changed. Life was so much simpler without the internet. We had to create our own imagination and make an effort in life. You had to; there was no other way to go through life.

Today everything is at our fingertip disposal and although some say not such a bad thing, it does bring with it the many fragile points in life, least not attracting many idiots and those in it for a quick scamming buck.

Many years ago I came across my first email scammer. It was allegedly from a Nigerian son of a diplomat telling me I was selected to be the recipient of a staggering 25 million US Dollars. I smiled then laughed. Of course I didn't believe it, why should I? I mean, out of the reported 7 billion people on this planet it was *I* who was selected by an African diplomat as his beneficiary.

First up, I have never been to Africa. Second, I have no relation whatsoever to any rich family, royalty, or elite group.

The emails later came thick and fast and as always, I like to make sport of really silly people and situations. It was my grandmother's phrase that inspired me to make a collection of these emails. In fact, it was not only her phrase but just about every grandmother in the Drumchapel area and later on in life I learned this phrase was actually universal: if an offer is too good to be true, it probably is.

It got me thinking as the emails came in. I wondered

ho my grandmother would have dealt with these emails and I wonder how my old neighbours would deal with them.

The following emails are actually real emails that I purposely selected for another book project but the replies are based on how my old neighbours and those wise ones from The Drum would react to them if they were alive today and active in the online world.

The E-mail:

Dear Sir/Madam, I wish to bring to your attention that you have been chosen to be the recipient of my father's will. My father passed away a few weeks ago and he left 20 million US Dollars in an offshore account. The problem is, none of us in the family can reach this money as we have restrictions in our country that forbids us. This is where you come in. You will receive 20% of my father's 20 million if you are kind enough to be our negotiated agent. To receive your 20% all we require is your bank details. Please note that this is not a scam and if you do not email me back within 7-days we will have to go elsewhere to look for a suitable candidate.

Sincerely,
(Name Supplied).

Mary's reply:

Dear *(Name Supplied)*,
I have to thank you, for taking the time to email me,

and I am very sad to read about the loss of your father. Before giving you my bank details I want to get to know you better.

Do you remember the film Scarface? Well, Tony Montana *(played by Al Pacino)* arrives at this gun-toting house to pay for and collect his cocaine. Unknown to Tony Montana, the so-called seller of the drugs was setting our Al up.

Anyway, I think the bandit's name was Hector, or something like that, *(don't quote me),* and he said to Montana after delaying the supposed deal: 'I just want to know who I do business with.'

That is the bit just before the chainsaw scene where there is blood everywhere. I mean, you should have seen it; it was a right mess. The guy gets slaughtered in the shower area…man, you could feel the blades as they churned inside of Montana's trusted sidekick.

The point I am trying to make here, *(name supplied)* is this: Like Montana's encounter with the drug dealer, I too want to get to know who I do business with.

Therefore, I would appreciate if you would take the time to write back to me and answer me the following questions:

 - What is your favourite cartoon character and why?
 - Do you prefer soda or tan tights?
 - What frightens you most about being tied up and attacked by a chainsaw? Do you wet the bed?
 - When one of your relatives hands you a new-born baby and you lovingly squeeze its little legs and you think the baby is so fecking cute; do you ever get the urge to sink your teeth into its wee cuddly fat arms?

I hope you don't mind but like Hector said, I like to know who I do business with.

Signed
Mary

Emailer:

Dear Friend,

I write to inform you that my aunt is dying of cancer and she cannot be treated or healed any more. The doctors have told her just to go home and rest in her house until she dies. This is tearing our family apart and I do not expect you to feel our pain but my aunt is very rich and is about to leave 15 million Dollars.

The problem is, our government will claim this money and use it for weapons against our people. We need someone in the United States or Great Britain with a personal bank account where we can send this money to.

The money will have to be in your account for one full month before we can send it back into our country. You see, my aunt's money cannot go from her account to any one of our family; it has to be funnelled through a US or UK bank then back into our country. That way our government cannot touch it. You will receive 10% of this 15 million and you can even keep the interest it will have accumulated in your bank. That's my family's gift to you. I hope you will return my email.

Best regards,
(Name Supplied)

Willie's reply:

Dear *(Name Supplied)*,

I am dreadfully sorry about your aunt's cancer. I

was wondering how close you were to your aunt because you never mentioned her name in your email. If I am to receive 10% of her 15 million I would really like to know her name. It's nothing special, I just want to be able to tell the guys in the pub when I drive up in my Rolls Royce who gave me the money. I can't very well say, 'Oh, this old lady from a country I cannot even pronounce just left me a fortune in her will.'

I am sure you will also understand my predicament when my wife finds out that a female gave me 10% of her 15 million. If you ever meet my wife you will know what I mean. She can be a really nasty piece of work when she is jealous…especially when she's on that *Special Offer* wine she buys at Tesco.

Oh, don't get me wrong, the money is not a problem—she will enjoy that, it's the woman issue. Some wives are loopy that way. For all I know, my wife will think the rich lady is the daughter of a rich banker and probably in her twenties with big t… Just one other thing, if you intend putting the money into my account for a month could you do it before Christmas? It's just that the kids want so much this year and as usual, it is our turn for the in-laws this time around and I would like to get them both something special like a house. Well, it will be a nice change from their usual socks and chocolates. Anyway, I sure hope you get back to me with your aunt's name.

Signed
Willie

Emailer:

Hi, I am the son of an African diplomat and I'm sorry to say he passed away recently. The reason why I contact you is to tell you that he left 480 zillion dollars in his will but cannot cash in on it unless it is shipped to a bank in another country. The thing is, I need your bank details including full account, sort code, full name of you and any other information you can supply us with to make this transaction smooth. From the 480 zillions my father's will is set at 20% to anyone who can store this money for a few short days until the rest of the family can flee the country.

Davie's reply:

No problem, Mr MWongo – or whatever your bloody name is – sounds like a great idea. You want my bank details and full contact/date of birth/and so on? And I only have to sit and wait for a few days until the money is processed into my account? This is great!

Let's break this one down for a bit, shall we? 480 zillion dollars with an attach of 20% for my provision. That would come to…let me get my calculator…jeez, my calculator doesn't have a big enough screen to tackle all those digits…*Wow!* It works…I'm due 240 000000000000!

I'll tell you what to do. Get a flight to Glasgow. I'll come and pick you up in a John Oliver's taxi and you can hand me the money in person. I like a wee handshake now and again and to be honest it'll get me oot the hoose.

Emailer:

Dear Sir or Madam,

Please do not ignore this email. I have some very important information that will make you rich. I have developed a formula that guarantees winning the lottery. All you have to do is send me 50 Dollars via the link provided and you will receive an instant download of the information in a PDF format. This works and has helped millions win the lottery.

Thank you;
(Name Supplied)

Renie's reply:

Nae bother, son. I'll just get my pension oot of my purse and hand it over to you but nae fear; according to you I am going to win the lottery with your guaranteed system so why should I care about a stingy 50-quid the government give me?

There's only one thing that bothers me, son. Why would you need all this money from possibly thousands of people when you have the formula to win the lottery yersel'? Wouldn't it be safer and more legal if you just used your own formula to win the jackpot instead of trying to take money from innocent and gullible people?

I'll make a deal with you. I'll give you my six numbers, you make me win the jackpot and I'll give ye yer 50-quid. How does that sound?

Signed
Renie

Betty's Bankster Call:

Betty would hate call-centres and telephone banking today. She was renowned for her tough-tackling and no-nonsense way of going through life, and she never shirked out of a conflict.

Having grown up in severe poverty and two World Wars there is no doubt all generations after her time would struggle to match her legendary script and how she dealt with people who she felt were trying to confuse or trick her.

The bank:

'This call may be monitored for training purposes. You are about to make a payment to your energy supplier. Please be aware by transferring funds from your bank account to your chosen recipient is solely your responsibility and any loss or damages which may or could arise from such a transfer is not the responsibility of us, your bank.'

Betty's reply:

'Listen, you here tae me, ya wee runt. I am funnelling through 80-quid and a few pence tae pay ma gas bill. It is *your* responsibility tae make sure ma dosh goes straight intae squaring up ma gas bill coz if ma heating gets cut aff, I'm gonnae come doon tae where you are and cut *you* aff. D'ye hear that?

Good, and I hope ye've still got yer wee listening monitor device thing on coz I've got mine on…for *my* training purposes.'

The call-centre:

Just after the September 11th 2001 attacks many banks sent out letters to members of their banks, requiring the account holders to fill in a form and send in copies of their identification documents. Many were business owners who lived overseas and account holders at home. What we now know now is it was just a way of building a grid and gathering even more information about us.

The then United States President, George W. Bush, was often heard repeating the famous 'Three Axis of Evil' countries, who he and his congress claimed were responsible for the attacks on the Twin Towers.

About a month later a former Drumchapel resident called his bank to be met on the other end of the phone by a voice speaking in a foreign accent that sounded awfully close to that of a person from one of the so-called Axis of Evil countries.

You couldn't make that one up.

Betty would have been fuming, had she been on the receiving end of that one. There is no doubt, knowing her persona and the language she'd use; she would have encountered huge problems that could easily have resulted in some sharp chest pains, swelling headaches and anxiety…for the person on the other end of the phone.

Call-centre: 'I am deeply sorry, M'am, but we need your password in order for us to proceed.'
Betty: 'I'm no tell ye. It's a secret.'
Call Centre: 'But I have to verify who you are.'
Betty: 'I jist telt ye. My name is Betty. B.E.T.T.Y.'

Call-centre: 'Okay, Betty, can you type in your password?'

Betty had difficulty remembering things. Her granddaughters always reminded her to write things down but security and privacy material is not what Betty would note down. It was always her thinking that all you need to know and remember should be inside your head. 'It keeps ye sharp,' she'd say. But passwords are not really in the front of the mind queue for remembering things. There were other more meaningful life situations that bore more importance like: surviving.

Call-centre: 'Okay, Betty. I am going to ask you a couple of security questions. What was your mother's maiden name?

Betty: 'She hud a few, son. She was born a Henderson, then flitted fae home tae home, then she wiz adopted. She then became Betty Smart afore the family who adopted her hud tae give her away as she wiz a bad lassie. So then she became a McLaughlin then changed her name tae Donaldson tae avoid a few debts. She got married tae a McCarthy but that marriage wiz a sham so she reverted back tae Henderson but by that time her name wiz never accepted as legal.'

The call-centre guy would be just too weak to keep up with Betty and Betty would not know there is a difference between the every day-to-day language to the one we have been so accustomed to over the latest years of fast-flowing technology.

She would, however, likely have her own call-centre

terms and jargon and she would be so right.

It might go a little something like this…

'Hullo, and welcome tae Betty's call-centre hotline. Your call is important tae me but before ye take part please read and accept ma terms.

Your call is being monitored right noo so that me and ma pals can huv a right laugh listening tae aw yous wee dafties during oor card school break.

If ye don't like ma terms ye know whit ye can dae. That's right. Get tae…'

Press (1) if ye want yer knittin' ripped by two dodgy Beethoven versions whilst wan of ma operators finishes polishing her nails.

Press (2) if yer skint and need a loan tae get ye through the weekend withoot the shakes.

Press (3) if ye want tae speak tae wan of oor sales personnel who will gladly sell ye a product or a service that's no worth a fuck and ye cannae afford it anyway.

Press (4) if ye would like tae be put on hold for another long sufferin' queue wait whilst we play a Karaoke version of The Birdie Song tae shred yer nerves intae confetti.

For all other enquiries: GO TAKE A FLYING FUCK!

Cyber Bullying:

As tragic as it is, try explaining cyber bullying to Willie, Mary, Jeanie and Archie; our dear old-time neighbours from former times. If they could come back, or we could go back in time, how would we break the news that kids can feel threatened by computer and mobile phone communication?

'Willie, you see, cyber bullying is when one or more persons makes a threat to another one or more persons over the internet. The internet is…well…I'll tell ye later. You can use a computer or a mobile phone to bully somebody. It's all the rage these days…er…excuse the pun.

'How does it work, son?'

'Ye jist log in tae yer account and start writing a bunch of explicit and slanderous messages to the person or persons you wish to read them. It's really that easy.'

'That's no bullying, son.'

'It is when they feel threatened. Ye can get the jail these days for that kind of stuff.'

'So how come they call it bullying if there is nae actual bullying taking place, son?'

'Well, tae be honest wi ye, there is bullying taking place. It is only verbal but people really feel hurt and some have even taken their own lives because of it.'

'Oh, my God, son. Really? That's terrible, son.'

'I know. It happens aw the time.'

'See in ma day, son, bullying meant a big stoater fae yer school and his cronies would round ye up in the playground, slap ye aboot, then take ye behind the sheds where the big stoater's cronies wid haud ye doon whilst the big stoater bully would kneel oan tap of ye and press something intae yer cheeks…like maybe…something lke…a SAWN-AFF SHOTGUN! And utter three words that would haunt ye for eternity: DINNER MONEY! That was bullying in ma day, son. Ye couldnae demand dinner money aff of somebody fae a distance. Ye hud tae pin them doon first.'

'I know, tell me aboot it. These days it's aw forward slash, semi-colon, I'm goonnae burst ye! followed by a closed parenthesis.'

'I can see this cyber bullying nonsense escalating intae a more non-contact way, son. In years to come, two teenage males will not be shouting out abusive threats in their normal silverback gorilla fashion, but instead, they will be waving furiously their iPhones at each other from opposite ends of the street; and it wouldn't surprise me at all if Apple decided tae see some prospective marketing advantages in this and develop an APP that you will be able to download and it will nae doubt be called the iChib. Whit a waste of a good future, son.'

Mary and Jeanie's Sales Assistant Encounter:

Can you imagine swapping time machine zones with our peers and take a trip into a modern day retail outlet?

Sales Assistant: 'Can I help you, ladies?'

Mary: 'No thanks, we're just huvin' a wee look around.'

Jeannie: 'Eh, haud oan a minute, hen. Maybe ye can help us. Ye can peel the tatties for the night's dinner;

there's a pile of washin' needin' hung oot, and some ironing tae be done, and whilst yer there ye can get the weans' school stuff ready for the morra.'

The Drum:
The Tragedies

Growing up in The Drum does not come without its tragedies and heartbreak. Throughout the book we've encountered humour and some light-hearted experiences but none of us can pretend – there were enough sad stories to go around.

There is no question this is by far the most difficult part of the book to read, as it has been to compile, but what would a Drumchapel book be without the people who made us who and what we are? As we say at the beginning of the book, the ones no longer with us are indeed the reason why this book was created.

It is also worth pointing out the amount of tragedies that have happened to Drumchapel families cannot all be documented. There are bound to be countless names missing but they will be remembered, be sure of that.

There are many family tragedies that stand out for the residents of Inchfad Drive. The mid-seventies was to see the sad loss of two very special mothers: Cathy Rankin and Agnes Grant.

It has always been common practise to name adults by their formal titles in Mr or Mrs but Cathy and Agnes were young women with young children and were extremely, extremely popular ladies.

The loss of both bore a huge hole in the hearts of the front closes of Inchfad, facing St Laurence's primary school, least not their broad horizon of family and extended family members.

The news was devastating. Not only were Cathy and Agnes so young; their untimely passing left a massive gap in many lives.

They were well-loved and highly thought of for their great parenting, but also the way they treated others around them.

Nothing was a problem for them. If you wanted your clothes altered or you needed somewhere to shelter until your own mum came back from the shops you knew where to go. Both Cathy and Agnes were made of traditional and upstanding stuff, never to be beaten.

When the news filtered through the closes, of Mrs Agnes Grant's passing, it hit us like a head-on collision. We couldn't believe it. We all knew she had taken quite ill but none of the neighbours expected what was to come. It was devastating, truly devastating.

The Grants were a family of envy, to most. They had everything you saw in the 70s TV shows. They were great kids; they were all good-looking, very well-behaved, and all good at what they did. They were the near-perfect combination. Gerry, Mark, Thomas, Barry and Lynne, were all St Laurence, and later St Pius students, but each of them will be remembered for their individualism.

Thomas was the star footballer, often starring for Spurs Boys' Club, and attracting attention. Mark was mature for his age, a very fine footballer, and was a great advisor to other kids. His authority in the street was evident. He didn't hold back any in an argument but he was a fair and top guy. Barry and Lynne were the famous twins. Being the youngest meant

Thomas, Mark and Gerry looked out for them a lot but like Mark, both Barry and Lynne were no slouches in holding their own.

Gerry was the oldest so the responsibility must have been huge for him to watch over the other ones but he carried that out extremely well. In all, the Grants were a family you wanted to be around.

To fully appreciate the Grants and their sense of humour you had to spend a Friday night in their house when the films came on…or rather…ended.

When the credits rolled for director, make-up, producer, and so on, the kids would cheer if their first name came up. As an example: if a film finished and the credits rolled and it read: Producer Thomas *Whatever,* young Thomas would claim one over the rest of the group and so on. It was always a safe and brilliant experience hanging out with the Grants. They were full of life and so it was even more sad when their mum passed away. All the kids were just too young.

Bill Grant, or, to give him his respected title, Mr Grant, was the father and head of the family. It must have been terrible for him to lose his young wife but somehow he managed. Strength like that has to be honoured, but it comes at a price. That New Year will never be forgotten. Mr Grant found what little comfort he could in the surroundings of the great Inchfad neighbourhood. Men don't really show emotions, or don't want to, but real men do. Mr Grant was allowed to and was encouraged to. What else could anyone expect when he had just laid his young wife to rest? He was in safe hands and he was loved and respected by all. I remember that night like it was yesterday. He looked shattered, as to be expected, as he gazed into his New Year's drinks glass; as if he was contemplating whether or not to take a drink or to just caress it. He looked undecided, or so it seemed. It was years later, much later, when it turns out he was trying his very best to keep his composure for the sake of the neighbours. He was an honourable and proud man and did not want to burden anyone. What a tragedy. How could Mr Grant be burdening anyone? I mean, here he was in the despair of all despairs and he was worried in case he upset the neighbours.

He buried his head in his hands. It was all-too-much. He was overcome and overwhelmed with sheer grief but what I do remember, looking back, was how close everyone was. In Inchfad it didn't require a tragedy to bring everyone together but with Mrs Grant's passing it showed how together the neighbourhood was. Everyone rallied round and comforted Mr Grant as best they could.

The Grant family were very close and being popular they had a lot of support in the neighbourhood. Later the kids all packed their bags for a trip to Germany to have a holiday with their relatives. It was a much-needed break for them and they deserved to have a smile on their faces.

We watched as they all set off for Glasgow airport. They looked completely different to the months previous, for the obvious reasons. It was just great to see the very first family most have us had ever seen set off for a holiday abroad. Morecambe was a stretch for most and the Grants will be the first to tell you about that excursion. It involved a train trip and their dog Patch who stayed behind but was well looked after by the Nicol family, up next close.

Tragedy turned to more tragedy just a short time later. Next close, and ironically, the lady who fixed up some amazing garments for the Grant kids for their trip to Germany, would pass away. Cathy Rankin, a lovely lady, like Mrs Grant, would leave behind a husband and children, at a very early age. It was yet another extremely difficult time for another well-loved family and again, the whole neighbourhood plunged into shock and despair.

Mrs Cathy Rankin was a strikingly good-looking woman. She looked like one of those film stars from the 40s classic movies. Her features, her shape, her dress sense, and the way she carried herself made her stand out above many. That being said, she was as down-to-earth and as humble as everyone else. She was immaculate and you would never think someone like her would be taken so early.

The neighbourhood rallied again for the sake of husband Tommy and the children, Helen, Lesley and young Tommy.

The Rankins were another lovely family. You could not imagine how much of a loss it was to such a nice bunch of people.

If the adults showed what it was like to unite then the kids would be given huge credit for what was to follow soon after Cathy Rankin's passing.

A couple of weeks after the tragic loss young Tommy and a group of kids were playing in the sand-pit over in the roaring fields that separated Drumchapel and the busy dual carriageway to the North. It was a normal wee boys' activity, when not taking part in their many games of football.

Tommy Rankin, Stephen Nicol, Thomas and Barry Grant, and a couple of other boys, were all living out their childhoods and playing in the sloping sand. Tommy was playing with a small yellow truck, making truck noises as he scraped the toy along the sand; creating his own little makeshift roads and world. Thomas Grant and Stephen Nicol were on the other side messing about and Barry floated between the boys and the other boys who were not really connected to the group.

There was no warning, no sign...nothing! Young Tommy was lying in the sand with his hands covering his face. He was screaming his poor heart out. He was yelling out for his mum. He was just uncontrollable. The grief overwhelmed him and from one second to the next he had gone from what looked like a happy wee boy to being reminded of the loss of his mum.

The other boys just stopped and stared for a few seconds before Thomas Grant quickly moved over to Tommy; lifting his sand-covered hands from his tiny face, then held him up. The other boys slowly moved across to help Tommy. It was horrible, truly horrible. For such a tragedy to happen to someone so young is really too sad for words.

The neighbourhood was used to sticking together. Thomas and Barry Grant knew all about losing their mum so they knew more than the other boys what it felt like for young Tommy. They all more qualified now in the terrible experience of grief.

Young Tommy gained his composure and the words from Thomas Grant was probably the best thing a child has said to another child. As he held Tommy up, Thomas, who was only a small handful of years older, said: 'Tommy, heid up, okay? I know what you are going through, I've been there; me and Barry have been there. Ye huv tae keep the heid up. Ye jist have tae get oan wi it, alright? We huv tae stick together, there's nothing else we can dae.'

Thomas' words made us all feel good but more importantly: it helped young Tommy Rankin get back up and soon after he was back playing with his wee yellow truck. Thomas showed, no matter if you are an adult or a child, you can always help another by helping them get through their most challenging times.

Tommy said himself that Barry Grant helped him cope, too. Tommy recalls sitting in the close with Barry, having their arms round each other, crying their wee hearts out and speaking about their mothers. They felt a lot better afterwards. Many of us learn that when we are adults – and some, like Tommy and Barry, had to learn how it feels to talk and feel better afterwards at an age when most of us were learning to ride a bike.

The same fate would return to haunt young Tommy in his adult life when his own kids lost their mother at a young age.

How cruel life can be.

The loss of a parent for any child is unbearable but the loss of a child, they say, is the most horrific life circumstance any mother and father could find themselves in. There have been many Drumchapel children taken so early in life from babies, toddlers and teenagers. They have passed on through illnesses and all-of-sudden tragedies.

The bus crash in which Girl Guides Catherine McKnight, Laura Cullen, Margaret Riddick, and Guide leaders Mary McGreskin and Rena Dougall tragically lost their lives coming back from a trip, shocked the people of Drumchapel. The scheme had seen its fair share of tragedies in the past but the now infamously named West Street Bus Crash became yet another sad and tragic part of Drumchapel and the people of Drumchapel.

There is a memorial garden dedicated to the girls and the leaders which has been extremely well-planned and groomed and a fitting icon for the Girl Guides and Girl Guides leaders. All five are often remembered and by the collective title of: *Angels.*

* Please note, it is impossible to publish a full account of all tragedies that happened to people from Drumchapel. These tragedies and the names of people in *The Drum* book have been written more from a personal account with connected knowledge and experience.

The Drum:
The Drum's Top Ten TV List

Watching TV with the auld neighbours has always been a tremendous experience and we can learn so much from how they see the world of make-believe entertainment.

The older generation don't do make-believe that well. They come from a world not known to a fantasy world like we know today. Back then it was all about survival. These days, people have time to fantasize.

'That Superman is a con, kin people no recognize him without his glesses oan?'

'That's actually a fair point. Clark Kent doesn't look that much different.'

'Aye, he's a chancer than yin, and they people are daft if they cannae see through him.'

'Naw, Willie, is it no Superman that can see through *him?'*

'Whatever the case, ye cannae con me wi takin' yer glesses aff, slappin' oan a bit of Brylcreem and getting' intae a pair of tights.'

In other films, where the plot actually looks like they've killed off the main star in the movie, can have cinema goers gasping. But not in The Drum.

Five minutes into a film the main actress looks to be left for dead. Not according to Mary. As she watches the film whilst ironing her man's shirt, she says,

'She's no deid.'

'How dae ye know that?'

'Coz, they've paid her a fortune. Dae ye think they are gonna pay her a fortune for five minutes work?'

'She might be deid. It could be the writers have

written her aff.'

'Nae chance. She gets up, springs back intae life then gets revenge oan that swine.'

As it turns out, Mary was right.

'How did you know that, Mary?'

'Ye think I'm daft? The film is based oan her. I've been watchin' films for years and they don't bump aff the big star that easy.'

How spot on Mary was. It is to do with life and our perceptions. They say you can learn so much from television but we can learn more by watching others watching TV.

'Haw Mary, I'm gonna send in my show idea.'

'Ach, away tae buggery. How kin you invent an idea for television?'

'I huvnae invented it. It's already a title.'

'Whit's it called?''

'It's called *Punch Yer Way Oot of a Wet Paper Bag.*'

'Who is gonnae buy that idea?'

'They could use it oan *It's a Knockout.* Ye jist get a bunch of guys fae the pub, make them take their shoes aff and get them tae step inside this big giant broon paper bag that has been hosed doon tae wettin' it. Then they huv tae punch their way oot it.'

Of course, when watching the telly there's always some smart arse who is willing to go that wee bit extra.

In hindsight, that's not a bad idea at all.

(((And for our next challenge, watch big Tam and his bawbag team from Glasgow, in Scotland, attempt to punch their way out of a wet paper bag)))

Dougie and Margaret's conversation is one of the favourites.

'I don't like those animal programmes, Dougie. The cheetahs are always chasing some poor animal then they eat them there and then, right in front of the cameras.'

'Margaret, whit d'ye think the cheetah was gonnae dae? Ye cannae watch a David Attenborough film where the cheetah uses its 75mph speed and technique for a few hundred yards jist tae jump on an antelope's back, then shag it.'

'See that wee Fred Flinstone, bye the way. He's my ultimate hero, so he is.'

'How's that?'

'Coz, he's the only guy who can still get things done aroon' the hoose by brandishing a club but no cause any injury; and he can put his fit through the flare of his caur and still pass an M.O.T.'

~ Big Chick ~

Growing up in The Drum and having the luxury of owning a television set meant a huge part of our lives felt a connection. There was no obsession way back then like 24-hour stations; we had three main ones, mostly, until another was added in the latter years before cable.

Black and white footage was what most residents got to see in the very early days. Television was not a necessity but a luxury few could afford.

It was a simple time for viewing. Stations then offered what many regard as the best-ever entertainment material and to this day a lot of it has yet to be rivalled, and it is unlikely it ever will.

In rounding up the research of what the people said about growing up in The Drum, a large part of it was based on their favourite memories but we extracted their mention of a favourite show or channel and came up with what can now call The Drum's all-time favourite television programmes.

10. Dixon of Dock Green

From the mid-fifties through until the mid-seventies, this very popular police drama became a household favourite that starred Jack Warner as the likeable 'bobby' who brought the nation some fine small-to-mid-level crime plots.

Frank McCafferty said of the show: 'Jack Warner was so known to us that we would use his catchphrase in the streets as kids, if we saw the polis. We'd whisper, 'Evening, all,' as a sign a copper was in the vicinity.'

Saturdays at tea-time in Drumchapel would see many a steamy window, half-drawn living-room curtains, and the flicker of a television screen; lightening up the condensation.

For many, Dixon of Dock Green equals the cosy winter nights where men and boys would stream off the supporters' buses and head home to the comfort of a steak pie and a nice warm cup of tea.

Right off the Celtic Supporters' bus, a young fan was met by a rival Rangers fan, but both knew each other.

'Paul! Get that hair cut, for fuck sake.'

'Nae chance. I'm growing it long and I'm no getting it cut until Celtic win the European Cup.'

'Ye'll huv longer hair than Rapunzel ya bampot, ye.

Celtic are no gonnae win the European Cup in your lifetime, or my lifetime…and I'm a lot younger than ye.'

The crimes on the show were light compared to the cop series' that would later follow but the 'ordinary copper' did punch it up a few notches as the years rolled on and into a world that came complete with more sinister overtures on the criminal market.

9. Opportunity Knocks

Hughie Green's face and voice was synonymous with the popular talent show contest. In The Drum the show was often referred to as Opporchancety Knocks (a slight tongue-and-cheek for chancers and their craving for fame and fortune).

The voting system used on the show would not pass in today's fast-moving society as the winner would be announced a week after the performance. 'In your own handwriting', was the earlier cry to send in your votes then the famous clap-o-meter was used for some of the decisions.

'Mr star maker himself, Hughie Green', would pop out from behind a curtain and unleashed future icons such as: Les Dawson, Pam Ayres, Peters & Lee and all the weans in The Drum remember with great fondness – Lena Zavaroni.

8. The Benny Hill Show

The Benny Hill Show was received worldwide but it also came with a lot of criticism with critics slating some of Hill's sketches as sexist. On the contrary it looked very much like some of the sketches involving scantily-clad women being chased by men; as more making sport of the silly-ness in the nature of men and their obsession with women.

Nevertheless, the show was long-running, hugely successful, and engrained in the memories of those who watched the fast-paced and various comedy material on offer.

It would be unthinkable, however, for some of the sketches passing through the political correctness and over-touchy liberals' conveyor belt of approval, today. You can't slap a young lady's backside for fear of being hauled up in front of a judge and the follically challenged would not take too kindly to the heavy-handed head slapping. Try any of the two in *The Butty* and you'd soon find yer heid 100-feet away in the swing park…with wee boys using it for a game of chippy in.

7. Love Thy Neighbour

If ever there was a television show that would never be aired in today's market it would have to be Love Thy Neighbour.

The show, as outstanding as it was, was never out of its critics' firing line.

The show was based around a stereotypical British working-class white couple with a black couple as their neighbours. Nothing unusual or untoward in that but the script content included language like, 'Sambo' and 'nig-nog'. A no-go in any generation.

But, the writing was brilliant and as equal in terms of the white guy and the black guy winning arguments and circumstances. The black neighbour used labels like 'snowflake' and 'white honky'. Both gave as good as they had and credit must be given to the balance in the script.

It was a brilliant show with lifelong remembering catchphrases, not linked to racism, like Eddie Booth's 'Bloody Nora!' 'Knickers', and 'The subject is closed.'

6. Starsky & Hutch

Loved by millions, watched by millions. The crime-busting duo is still described to this day as the best cop show ever to be aired on television. Fans of other shows like Kojak, Ironside and Z-Cars might disagree but there is no arguing about the quality and the chemistry Paul Michael Glaser (Starsky) and David Soul (Hutch) had on the screen.

The show will forever hold a dear place in the heart of youngsters growing up in The Drum. Who didn't want to be as cool as Huggy Bear? And who never fantasized about owning a red Gran Torino with a white lightning strip?

A couple of Ford Capris and even a Granada were spotted hovering around Drumchapel, circa 1976. We have no idea who the owners of the vehicles were or if they even came from Drumchapel, but fair play for the attempt...and the bad paint job.

There were indeed a few Huggy Bears in The Drum, but that's for another story.

5. Eurovision Contest

Not weekly but an annual show, the Eurovision Song Contest was a popular choice amongst our *People from The Drum's Favourite Telly Shows.*

Mostly, the popularity in our survey was based down to childhood memories rather than for the musical greatness; with perhaps the exception of ABBA.

That image of the group and the intro to the now classic hit *Waterloo* came only second in our survey to Brotherhood of Man's *Save Your Kisses for Me*, followed by memories of Bucks Fizz and their song *Making Your Mind Up*. Although, to be honest, the Bucks Fizz song sprung to mind mainly due to the ripping off of the skirts during their 1981 Eurovision performance. And the fact the shows had now travelled from Drumchapel and parked their trucks and rides over at the football pitches on the Linvale end, near the fly-over on Great Western Road.

'Haw, Billy, wid ye pump they two fae ABBA?'
'Aye, Ah wid, and Ah wid pump their wives, anaw.'

4. Coronation Street *(the older version)*

Not surprisingly the all-time favourite soap from the 60s and 70s came out on our Drum Top Ten TV Shows.

Not one of our survey people mentioned Coronation Street from the 80s to present day. All the women in the survey said Coronation Street was at its peak in the earlier years until it started to get silly.

For those in their 40s the tune and the cat on the roof was their most vivid memory.

For those in their 50s it was Hilda Ogden's hair net that sparked the nostalgia.

3. Bless This House

Sid James and Diana Coupland will be forever remembered as the couple with the two teenage kids and plenty of side-splitting laughs.

Although set in England, the folks from Drumchapel cold relate to the show for its down-to-earth cast, set, and characters.

At its height it was one of the most popular TV shows in the sitcom genre.

2. On the Buses

One of the funniest and entertaining shows and it's no coincidence it sits nicely parked at our number 2 spot.

The characters are legendary and the writing must be given all the credit for turning out a classic after classic from a bus station and bus driving template. Absolute genius. It would have been great if they'd filmed on the number 20 route.

'Haw, Butler, make ma day and take me tae the Lincoln, ya daft arse, ye.'

1. Some Mothers Do 'Ave 'Em

Who could ever forget Frank Spencer and his wife, Betty? What is most surprising is the show was voted in a list of best British sitcoms but it didn't score as high as our Drum poll. This is down to a mixture of who we asked and what made people laugh the most.

Michael Crawford and Michele Dotrice became a

household duo but it was Crawford's character and his range of catchphrases that made him the most impersonated TV character at that particular time.

'Ooh! Betty', he would say, holding his finger to his mouth and glaring a glaeckit look.

Swirly wallpaper, matching carpet & plastic bathroom tiles
Saturday morning cartoons with wide open smiles
Osmonds' number ones and coming home late
Babysitter giving out rows for staying out late – until way past eight

Stealing adult cups of tea
Hero cops winning always on our TV
A ride in uncle's Vauxhall Viva
Mother singing at a wedding, like a Pop Soul Diva

Patterned shirts and pointed collar
Looking back on your first wedding day shots and wondering why you ever did bother
Learning the trade of cute schoolboy charm
But feeling for the first time – a policeman's firm arm

Hunting down birds' nests
Auntie has failed another one of those driving tests
Owning a telephone if you were working
Working only if you were looking
Avoiding toothache only when you were sooking

Hot pants in the street
Hot gossip in the neighbours' below
Glam Rock pumping out of the stereo

The Drum: *The People's Story*

These are just some of my fondest memories
of the 1970s

Summer school kids, screaming and trashing dustbins
without the lids
Plastic toy soldiers in miniature
Sharing blankets between 5 – constantly itchin' ya
First taste of a McDonald's milkshake
Long lost relatives from Canada's firm handshake
Families gathering, the excuse for a party
Emptying the shelves at the off license; 100 bottles of
beer
And a half bottle of Bacardi

Kitchen worktops in tablet beige
Sitting on my dad's knee watching a newsflash episode
of the Balcombe Street siege

These are just some of my fondest memories
of the 1970s

Adults were 18
Horror films way back then were frighteningly
frightening
German measles; that excruciating childhood bug
Leaving tiny faces looking like a Persian rug

Fresh bakers' crust
Adults we could trust
Summer storms and the struggle to stay warm
Children's moment of innocent pleasure
Grinning like a pirate who's just found his treasure

Those wonderful days that meant so much

Tons of episodes of my heroes Starsky & Hutch
Combat/The Six Million Dollar Man/Charlie's Angels
and Saturday nights with Dick Emery
Sadly those days are all but gone but I'd like to thank
them all for giving me my fondest memories…

…of the 1970s

The Drum:
School Trip & a Burns' Tale

It was announced our class were to take a trip to Burns' Cottage. We were all ages of eight and nine so the chances of us ever knowing who Burns was, or is, would be extraordinarily remote.

In the run up to the trip it was our grandparents who were more excited about the prospects of the grandweans going to the sacred house where the great bard and his family lived.

As it turns out, the New Year parties we had in The Drum brought us closer to Burns but we didn't know he lived in a wee hoose. We just thought it was a song. Well, it wasn't a song you'd hear on the radio that often but Rabbie Burns was, to us weans, a mysterious guy with sideburns, a fluffy shirt collar and he looked quite odd, if you want the truth. He didn't look like an icon who wrote poetry.

The trip to Burns' Cottage was the very first one I ever took part in at Drumry Primary. Half the coach was full of my class and the other half was filled with boys and girls from another class, but the same age-group.

The only bus a lot of the kids had been on before was a number 9, a 20, or a 19. For the more adventurous ones, the blue bus was as about the closest some got to the feeling of going somewhere exotic. Some kids in my class had never been on a coach before and some had only been on one as they headed to places like Millport for a holiday. Supporters' buses don't count.

I was lucky enough as I had been on trips before so

it was not a new thing for me.

We all waited in the classroom all ready to go. The excitement was unbearable and the teacher and her assistant were struggling to contain us. The word came through that the coach had arrived at the Abbotshall entrance.

We were led out by a couple of teachers in our usual line-up of twos. It was always encouraged to have a boy and a girl together but sometimes the sides didn't add up and some were sneaky enough to line-up beside their best pals. Willie Robertson and I were good friends and we walked out of the class and onto the coach as a team. Willie grabbed the best seat on the bus and we couldn't stop admiring the high seats. It was a new coach and the smell of the new interior really made us feel we were going on a long and expensive journey. I have no idea how much the parents paid – if they did at all – but we felt special. The school never held back any and neither did the teachers because we were well-fed and my best memory about the trip was when the teacher came round us all passing out the sweeties. The suspension on the bus was like something you'd find on a carnival ride. The teacher walked from the front of the bus to the back handing out the goodies; holding onto each seat head as she did. She looked like an air hostess juggling hot coffee in mid-air turbulence as she made her way back to her seat.

We sang songs, we laughed, we swapped seats and we all grabbed the chance to look out of the rear window of the coach as often as we could. We weren't rowdy but you have to imagine about a quarter of that coach had never seen the inside of such a vehicle, never mind take a ride in one. It was just an innocent trip to Ayrshire but one that was the first for many.

We had no idea where we were going. It was an educational trip but for us we didn't know if we were heading North, South, East or West.

When we arrived it was like another country. There were other bus and coach loads of school kids from all over the country. Most of the kids from other schools were kitted out in their full uniforms. Our dress code on this particular trip was optional and as a result of it being optional; I don't recall many, if any, who wore a school tie. We were meant to feel as comfortable as possible but we were not allowed to wear our out-of-school clothes. There was some form of dress discipline and I remember the teacher's letter she gave to us prior to the trip with a list of things to do and not to do. The main one was we were allowed to dress without our uniforms but remember, we are representing the school and Drumchapel. In hindsight it was probably a bit of psychology to inform us we were representing The Drum. Subconsciously the parents must have thought, 'Aye, we'll show them who is the best,' because we were all pretty much well-dressed and fit for any representative purpose. We didn't let the school down and we were proud of ourselves of where we came from.

One school party we met wore wee funny school uniforms. The blazers were bright purple, their shorts (yes, shorts) were stiff grey and they all had neatly-pressed socks. What killed us was their wee hats. They looked like the kids in the Curly Wurly advert. Some of the kids were huge, just like Terry Scott's character in the famous advert. They were from England and they just looked different to us. They were fantastic looking but we were just as important and just as well-behaved. They had been on trips before. Their experience just showed. Some of our kids looked like they had dropped in from another planet. That being said, as the Curly Wurly advert boasted, we out-chewed everything for 3p.

We were given the tour of Burns' Cottage and at our age it is appreciated we didn't really get his words but we all had a great time when we went into where Burns used to live. It just looked really weird and small. The only houses we were used to in another world were the *Peter and Jane* books but we'd never been in their house. This was just incredible to be in a house of a famous person.

We were encouraged to ask as many questions as possible about Burns but we didn't start asking the teacher or the guide any until we were in the cottage.

'Miss, where is he the noo?' a wee girl's voice echoed in the tiny stone-clad room.

'He died a long time ago,' replied the teacher.

'But his bed's jist been made. Is his maw still alive?'

'Don't be stupit! He died hunners o' years ago. If he's deid, his maw will be deid,' a wee boy's voice replied.

The teacher must have been having a laugh at some of the questions but she must have been glad the trip was not a waste of time.

We were ushered out of wee Rab's bedroom to make way for another party of kids. We couldn't get away with the size of the house. The ceiling was really low and all the furniture seemed to be fit for really small people. The teachers were great, it has to be said. They taught us in such a way that it was interesting. One of the adults who accompanied us told us how people lived back in those days. He was not a teacher or a guide but perhaps a parent or grandparent. I have no idea who he was but I do remember the conversation really well as he tried to explain to a few of us outside in the gardens.

'The people in the auld days were wee folks.'

'Did they no grow any fae when they were oor age?' a wee girl asked.

'No really, hen. Most people were wee and they didnae live as long as we dae noo.'

'How no? Did they no eat aw thur dinner?'

'They didnae really huv big dinners or a lot tae eat so anything they did huv put doon tae them they wid be scoffin' it as it might be the last dinner for a few days.'

'Did they no huv any puddin'?' a wee voice from the back of the crowd asked.

'I don't know, son. It was hard enough jist tae huv a dinner.'

'We're lucky then coz we get a puddin'.'

'Aye but jist oan a Sunday,' a wee boy shouted.

The crowd of boys and girls just chuckled with laughter. It was the beginning of a comedic life for all of us. Even at a young age we all knew what it meant to have a laugh and not many kids were short of a wee bit of ad-lib. At 8-years-old, remarks like that were way beyond their years.

Willie Robertson and myself signed the guest book as we left. We were both too young to think about any future but we did say we would come back when we were older and see our names.

249

I am not sure if Willie did return but I did on two occasions. In 1993 and in 2004. I didn't see my name in the guest book as it was probably a new guest book but apart from a bit of refurbishment, the cottage looked like it did in 1973. Of course, that wouldn't be that difficult as it was the cottage wee Rabbie lived in hundreds of years ago.

That whole day in Ayr was just terrific. It was all we talked about for weeks after. The trip back home was relaxing. Some of us fell asleep. It was a long day and the fresh air knocked us out. The suspension of the coach and the clean seats made for a great kip all the way up the road.

At New Year and each Burns' Night I don't think of the bard and his lyrics. I think of the trip on a smooth coach and the teachers for giving us a day out to remember: for the rest of our lives.

In 2008 I was asked to write a script for an after dinner speakers' night at a Burns event. When you get asked to write a comedy sketch for a Burns' Night you know you must be good, must be informed about Burns, and have a gift of telling a Burns' tale. I qualified for none of the aforementioned but I did draw my inspiration from my trip to the cottage as an 8-year-old and to me, a Burns' tale would not be complete without him being related in some way to The Drum. I don't care how international Rabbie Burns is and it doesn't interest me how many countries sing Auld Lang Syne, or how many languages it has been translated into; a Burns tale, for me, has to be fae The Drum.

A Burns' Tale:

I couldn't help but wonder what the great bard would make if he lived in the world we live in today. What, with all this political correctness stifling our very speech; what would he make of all this? Do you think he'd get away with, 'Wee sleekit, cow'rin, tim'rous beastie'? The Language Enforcers *(PC Brigade)* would most likely curb that sentence into a more appropriate European Union legislated, 'Vertically challenged mammal belonging to the rodent species.'

And he wouldn't be afraid, he'd simply be, 'Bravely Disoriented'. The poor creature wouldn't even be allowed to be called a wee white mouse: he'd be labelled Caucasian.

How would Burns earn his living in this thriving urban environment? Would he be an unemployed ploughman or to merge his lowland vernacular with the proper Byres Road English – would he be unemploughed?

Actually, to be honest, when you take into consideration that he was, after all, a man and a man for o' that; he hasn't really changed or evolved to keep up with ever-increasing changes in society. I'd say he'd just be like most men today: a lazy so and so who only marry so that they don't have to hold their stomachs in anymore and for the real lazy so and so's; they only go jogging to get rid of some of that excess waistline; you know…just enough so that their bellies don't jiggle when they use a lawnmower.

How would Rabbie cope adapting from the feathered pen to the current day lyrical instruments poets and writers have in this modern society? How the hell would he be able to work out when he's ran out if invisible ink?

His language was beautiful, his words, his works and the whole twang of it is probably as arousing to the women as French call-centre girls are to the modern man; but living today – if he was to find himself in amongst this service industrial city – he'd need to change the lowland accent to a more Gleswegian rumble. Surely he wouldn't get away with words like, 'awa' and 'bonnie lass', up in The Drum?

Can you imagine his mum sending him out for some good old-fashioned Glesga errands and wee Rab was to find himself queuing at the local butchers. I can just see Rab right now – of course, moving to Glasgow he'd have to first get rid of that Rabbie stuff and adopt oor short sharp and to the point and better way to address a Robert. I can just see our young bard muttering away under his breath trying out our local dialect before ordering. As the butcher backs out of his freezer and stands in front of his paraffin heater with hands behind his back, wee Rab would look at the bloody red meat through the glass shelves and in his native tongue he'd ask the butcher, 'Is that yer Ayrshire bacon?' to which the Glaswegian butcher would most likely answer, 'Naw, son, am jist heatin' ma haunds up.'

Now, Burns' side-kick, Tam O'Shanter – there's a man who'd help oor Rab settle into our modern lifestyle without any problems. He has so much in common with Glaswegian men. A guid night oot downing a few hard strong ale refreshments on this side of the equator has resulted in many a Glasgow man to cry to his wife that on the way back fae the pub he was chased doon the street by a ghost on a white horse.

You have to admire the way oor bard and his family lived, though. Can you imagine returning the compliment of our bard-exchange by sending one of oor Glaswegian bard-ish pale reflections down the coast to live the Burns way? I don't think any of the contemporary male half of the population would last the length of a quick Rabbie verse, match his smouldering personality and come to think of it: I don't think any of our contemps would even last a length.

Perhaps only one fully-grown man with any gile could live the Burns way and that'd be my own granddad. He could certainly keep up with bard in the drinking sense and not so much as a womanizer as oor Rab himself. My granddad, however, is no stranger to the wit and ad-lib the bard is synonymous with. But, I hasten to add, I doubt any man could live through the harsh winters on the fields with the ploughmen. Never mind keeping up with the Jones's – it'd be more like heating up wi the Burns's.

Supposing we caught the present day reality TV bug and showed a family swap series whereby my granddad was to live with Rabbie's family and Rabbie was to live with my family in Drumchapel. My granddad would go for a few tankards down at the local ale-house as Rabbie so often enjoyed and he'd come sauntering home through the marsh and heather in the wee sma' oors. At first dawn he would need to rise very early to plough the fields (at the same time Rabbie would be tucked under a Marks & Spencer's duvet waiting on his fortnightly cheque that rhymes with Rabbie's biro). Mrs Burns would prepare a hearty breakfast of tripe and onions washed down by a gallon of sheep's runny cheese milk.

The clothing would not be your ready-made retail garmentry and hard leather boots that awkwardly lace up the same way no matter which way yer facing.

As my granddad would struggle with the right boot trying to put on his left foot and the left boot squeezing uncomfortably onto his right foot, Mrs Burns would yell at my granddad in her broad and commanding Ayrshire whail, 'Ach fur God's sake, son, ye've goat yer bits on the wrang feet!'

In a turn of modern-day quick-witted Glaswegian back-chat, my granddad would quip back, 'Aye, yer effin' right there doll…they should be oan *yours!*'

Young Rabbie would be by this time enjoying his new exchange life up in the comfortable west end and soon he'd be accompanied by his good old drinking buddy, Tam O'Shanter. You have to understand that it would be too much of a culture shock to hit them too quickly with the bright lights and swanky pavements so they'd be staying in digs up in Drumchapel first just to get them used to their new way of life.

Taking a Saturday afternoon trip down Byres Road to break themselves into this new modern world they find themselves in; I can't help but wonder what on earth they'd think of the swish coffee shops and up-market ale-houses; green, white and gold double-decker carriages with the names of their destination displayed on the front of them –

whizzing by; with people upstairs smoking and people downstairs reading outstretched newspapers. Come to think of it, what about the little shops that sell the lottery tickets?

'Tam, c'moan in and see if we can win 16 million of these funny wee green and brown notes wi a picture of a strange man dressed up as a wummin on them.'

'Naw, Rabbie, ye widnae want to win all that money. I mean, whit aboot aw they begging letters?' 'Ach, Tam, dinae worry yersel seek, we'll jist keep sendin' them as normal.'

As my granddad would be stretched out knackered on a field, the hunger would set in. Knowing him as I do I can picture him soldiering on into the village to the nearest ale-house for a quick bite and refreshment. He ate a Ploughman's lunch and washed it down with four pints of McEwan's lager. As you can imagine both weren't too happy with my granddad and proceeded to set about him.

Back up in Byres Road, Rabbie and Tam O'Shanter decide to take part in the Glesga ritual of an *aw day shot*. Drinking the afternoon away until finally they headed up to Cleopatra's for a richt guid shindig *(as they thought it would be).*

Inside Cleo's, Rabbie and Tam find themselves sitting in a waltzer seat surrounded by disco mirror balls and…well…wall-to-wall mirrors.

'Hey Tam!' Rabbie shouts, over three octaves of Gloria Gaynor, intrigued by the mirror images returning to his receptive and curious eyes, 'that guy over there is the spitting image of yersel.'

'Christ, so he does, Rabbie, c'moan ower and see if they want a wee dram wi us.'

As Rabbie & Tam get up, Rabbie turns to Tam and

says, 'Ach, dinnae bother, they've seen us, they're baeth comin' ower tae us.'

As the night wears thinner, Rabbie and Tam find they've no money for a horse-and-cart and not accustomed to taxis they decide to head off to the nearest bus depot in Great Western Road.

As Rabbie is the bravest he knicks inside to steal one of those big double-decker carriages and Tam waits outside to alert Rabbie if the polis come. Rabbie's been in the depot for about fifteen minutes when Tam shouts in, 'Rabbie! Christ's sake, whit's keepin' ye?'

Rabbie's filtering echoey voice shouts back, 'Ah cannae find wan that says DRUMCHAPEL oan it.' Tam, ever the impatient one, tries to shout back quietly, 'Well jist get wan that says KNIGHTSWOOD and we'll get aff and walk the rest.'

After the family swap exchange fortnight my granddad finally came home a little bit worse for wears. It was not for him. I should have sent my granddad's pal because he was used to rough conditions like that. He was a POW – a *Prisoner of War* – and he used to tell me some frightening stories about being captured in Japan.

'What was it like being a POW in Japan?' I asked him.

'Well, actually, son, the weather wiz atrocious but the food was no too bad.'

My granddad had similar Burns' experience-type stories when he came back from boot camp (the right on the left and the left on the right, remember?) Apart from the hard-working and living conditions my granddad was most intrigued by how they celebrated parties and events down Burns' way. It was so different from those up in Invercanny. He's never heard so many bagpipers all at the same time.

'So how would you sum their entertainment skills, granddad?'

'Well, to be honest with you, blowing the bagpipes is a bit like throwing a javelin blindfolded through a close in Dunkenny...in the dark. You don't need to be that good at it to get people's attention.'

The Drum:
The Babysitters

The nature of the population age of Drumchapel proved to be a scattering of very young and the elderly. There was no such term as a new town in the respect of age. It may have been a new scheme but many families brought with them their older loved ones from the inner-city.

Many families had very young toddlers and the grandparents in the same house and of course, as we all know, the level of entertainment in The Drum was never short.

Cue in the need for some very, very important people who have to be given the same credit as all the unsung heroes: the babysitters.

Husbands and wives and partners worked and lived hard so the need to unwind and let their hair down meant someone would be recruited for a couple of bob to look after the weans. If the grandparents or neighbours were not available the babysitters were given the adult roles of watching the kids.

In our street we had Helen Rankin, Bibby Conlan, Janey Johnston, Celia and Maureen Deans; and the Vernon sisters, Catherine and Sandra. They were pretty much the same age, or as near as, and would take great pleasure in babysitting for the weans. Helen Rankin was many a favourite with the kids but they were all great babysitters. Catherine and Sandra Vernon lived above me in my close and Sandra babysat for me and my sister on many occasions. Sandra said: 'I loved to babysit but it wasn't because you were good kids; it was because your mum worked in Beattie's biscuit factory and I was allowed to help myself to the biscuit tin.'

Celia and Maureen lived directly next door to me and both sisters were a great laugh and you never knew what they were up to next. They did babysit for us on numerous occasions and like all the other girls they brought with them a brilliant night of entertainment but they were also strict and took their responsibilities seriously and well.

Not all babysitting happened inside a house. For short emergencies we would be allowed to play in the street near the close but we were never allowed to venture out of sight. Mr & Mrs Deans seemed to be the ones who would gladly look out for us on these occasions. They were strict and they commanded that respect thing that you only get with really great people.

They had a fixed eye and they never left that window. They were a great family in our street and I can still see Frank with his Celtic scarf going to and coming back from games. If you needed a family to look out for you and look after you it was the Deans.

Sandra and Catherine were incredibly funny. They were a comedy duo but the whole family were entertaining. I've often written and spoken about the Vernons and the talent they had in the family. Music seemed to have been their biggest asset but all the family had something that was instantly likeable. Brian, Stewart, Stevie, Catherine, Sandra and Lynne were all what we used to call, *The Drumchapel Partridge Family.*

Bibby Conlan was another girl who was very popular and I remember the nights she babysat for us. Bibby (Elizabeth) was allocated a Thursday and of course Thursday nights were Top of the Pops nights. Bibby would bring a couple of her friends and they would sing and dance to some of the tracks played on the programme. They were big Bay City Rollers fans. After Top of the Pops they would whip out their records and play them. We were allowed to stay up a wee bit later than normal but our parents knew this and were in agreement. The responsibility the girls had was obvious and although they were teenagers who liked to have fun, they were also very responsible and reliable. Not one time did anything go wrong under their watch and a good reason they were always asked to come back. The pocket money for the girls came in handy but they were mature for teenagers. They were also in demand and the competition – although they never looked at it this way – meant they had to be good at what they did. There was enough kids in the area and plenty of babysitting opportunities. It was very tight but credit to all the girls; they were all extremely good at babysitting and they were also very nice people.

We must have given them some grief with our cheek, I am certain of that, but I'm quite sure if they are reading this they will be complimentary to us kids but not as much as we compliment and appreciate them.

Bibby's babysitting nights were louder than the others but in a good way. She was strict but she enjoyed her music, her friends and their company. A very bubbly character. We were allowed to watch Top of the Pops with the volume higher than normal and we were allowed to play records but once it was bedtime she meant business.

Helen Rankin was the softer nature of all the babysitters. She was quiet but very firm. She ran her own dance class in the St Laurence's school so she knew the meaning of discipline and was not afraid to instil it. Helen's babysitting nights were great experiences. She too, loved her music and let us stay up a wee bit later. Helen was a very responsible babysitter and great fun to be around. Kids would follow her around, such was the impact she had in the community.

Janey Johnston babysat on many occasions. She was more strict, but again, all babysitters had to be. The responsibility was enormous, looking after someone else's children. Jane was a commanding figure and she took great pride in entertaining the kids in the street. Another bubbly character who had a firm hand in keeping things together but she was also up for having a laugh and taking part in many of the activities and games in the street. She was someone you preferred to have on your side.

Sandra Vernon was the closest, as she lived upstairs from us. She was a hilarious girl, full of life and fun. It was always a giggle when Sandra came to babysit. The first thing she did when our parents left the house was claim pole position for the seat closest to the television set and she was not slow in cuddling that biscuit tin. You had to rugby scrum it from her. Her sister Catherine was not far behind. She'd come down the stairs in her slippers, make sure everything was alright then get stuck into the tin.

It was more common for the babysitters to come to the houses where the kids lived but as most of us lived up closes it wasn't too uncommon for the kids to go to the babysitter's house. One particular occasion was at Halloween in the mid-seventies when both my parents were working their shifts and I had a Halloween party at the 77th B.B. in Drumry Primary. What was about to unfold (literally speaking) is still a talking point to this very day, and especially when Halloween comes round.

I had no idea what to dress up as. The previous year I was a pirate and never won a prize because there were about ten pirates on show. Allow Catherine and Sandra Vernon. The following was an example of creative brilliance and how we made up our own little world at times. We sat in the living-room with an hour to go before I was to set off on the walk to the Halloween party. The kids were a step ahead of me as they were already out on force and there were a couple of dookin' for apple parties already shelved for later on. I am not sure how or why this came up but Catherine and Sandra used a pile of bandages from the cupboard in their house and started to wrap them around me; covering me head-to-toe. I was now officially an Egyptian Mummy.

They both walked me to the school in the dark and I have to say we turned heads and scared a few people. I won first prize but I was unrecognizable. I had to verify my association with the 77th B.B. because I could have been anyone walking in off the street.

In a conversation not long ago, after many years, Catherine and Sandra brought up that Halloween night as if it happened the week before. I still find it really amazing anyone could remember that event but all credit to Catherine and Sandra Vernon for showing some great initiative as only a couple of kids from The Drum could come up with.

I would not say it has been topped and not even equalled but that night, and with the help of Catherine and Sandra, I used that experience to my advantage when I won first prize in a Halloween costume as an adult. I did not dress as an Egyptian Mummy. I could never recreate the magic that Catherine and Sandra made that Halloween night. It did, however, make me alert to the facts of being creative and pulling hats out of rabbits. I dressed up as a police frogman. I had the snorkel, the suit and the flippers. I even had seaweed and a rusty bike with buckled wheels tied to me. It was a mess but I won first prize. It did have its drawbacks, though, because I was with a party of couples and I couldn't get a round of drinks in. Not because people were standing on my flippers but because there was *ten-deep* at the bar.

The Vernon girls were famous for their antics. They were just great fun but again, the responsibility in watching someone else's children was high but the Vernon girls, like Bibby, Helen, Janey and all the other girls who were famous for their babysitting skills, were all good at what they did.

May King was another babysitter who babysat for Fergus Russell. I am not sure where she came from but she was connected in some way to Fergie's mother. It could well have been a bakery thing but May was a nice girl and great company to be around.

Back in the 70s a lot of people worked shifts so it was important to keep the stability in families and babysitters played a huge and important role in the community of Drumchapel. The Goodyear Club, the

Golden Garter and the many community hall events for adults only, meant the weans had to stay at home and nobody was better equipped to look after us than The Drum babysitters.

In all the time of our babysitting experiences I can honestly say there was never a time when a thing went wrong. I am not sure about leaving kids in today's world but if I had the chance I would have any one of those girls looking after my kids because they would look after them very well – as they certainly looked after us.

The Wean: Lynne Vernon

Helen Rankin in her famous dance pose

The Drum:
The Playgrounds

The Adventure Playground was most notably known for its stationary boats and canon; and the playground at the north end of Inchfad Drive was famous for its monkey bars, but the shopping centre swing park (as it was often known as) was easily the most frequented play area for kids and adults, alike.

The impressive putting green, the modern tennis courts, and the plush bowling green all made up for a gathering of all generations. The summers were magnificent and full.

Adjacent to the park the adults could enjoy a refreshment in the Hecla Arms as the kids took advantage of the grass space, shoot slide, swings and the roundabout and spider roundabout.

The playground in Inchfad was built mid-seventies having replaced lock-up garages.

There were many areas where kids congregated. Drumchapel had so much open space it was almost as if it was designed purely for children.

Recreation was never short of facilities. The community spirit of Drumchapel people is evident from the amount of halls and centres. From the Kinfauns Centre to the Community Centre were just some of the places the folks from The Drum would meet for discussion and activities. Churches, Chapels, schools and huts (the scout hall) all had open doors and welcomed anyone from the area and were also very good at welcoming guests from afar.

Halgreen was potentially a superb place for a

football arena of some sort. It had the size and the shape. There were a couple of grass pitches with metal goals but for years the pitches were not used in the manner in which they could and should have been used.

There was a small playground near the school gates of Drumry Primary and the nursery at the other end was full of young life.

Across the pitches there were a few paths that were carved out by taking a short cut to and from school and the grass, although well-kept by the council, had seen its better days after bonfire night and the side-ups the football kids would take part in.

The pitches must have shown some potential because the army would use it for their displays. It was now what we call marketing and a recruitment means but it was entertaining. The bangs from the artillery were real and not just a couple of lame twangs from a spud gun. Those bangs were frightening.

In fairness the army brought with them a well-drilled and very organized unit, as you would expect, but if they were asking me to join up I would have said no because those bangs put me off. I was way too young and this would have caused a different affect but many young men and women joined the military from Drumchapel and served their country and time well. I am not sure if the army display was successful in recruiting anyone at that time but for what it's worth they sure put on a great campaign; if that was their goal.

The crowds that gathered were treated to real life-like action and this was not a film they were making. Those tanks and equipment were not props; they were finely-tuned and well-oiled machines in superb working condition.

It was a balmy tea-time when a crowd of young men gathered on the sloping hill on the Abbotshalll side of the pitches. A couple of officers were going around talking to the young men when one of the guns fired a loud bang. It was deafening. It made your heart stop. From the crowd one of the officers had just asked one of the group of young men how he felt about joining the army. Just a second after the bang the young man said, 'Fuck that, for a game of soldiers.'

He later joined up.

The Drum:
Sleepwalking in Drumchapel

In my adult years I found myself in a bar in downtown Toronto, in Canada. I would be met by a person who would clear up a childhood situation of mine that has enthralled and haunted me at the same time.

I stood at the bar watching a baseball game on the pub screen. I had no interest in any sport other than the fitba. 'If it's no a size 5 baw it's no fir me,' I used to say.

I have no idea how I ended up in this particular bar as I was not a pub person, as such, but what happened would please the *it's meant to be* crowd.

An American Indian gentleman put his hand on my shoulder and called me Sleepwalker. He officially gave me that title and it stuck. Coming from Drumchapel you don't meet many Indians. I have to point out that Indians in America prefer Native American to Native Indian. They were there long before most so they have earned their rights; or whatever rights they still have as most have been taken from them; but that's for another history lesson.

I was suspicious of him but not scared. I was more curious as to why he called me Sleepwalker.

'How do you know I used to sleepwalk?'

'I just know. You have a history of sleepwalking, right?'

'Aye, as a matter of fact, aye. I used to sleepwalk quite often. But how did you know?'

'I can feel your wandering spirit,' he said, in a cool

and laid back film-like tone.

Someone must have told him or sent him. I admit, I have family in Toronto and other places in Canada but I have no recollection of any of my family having a connection to Native Americans. It must be a wind-up, right?

There was nothing creepy about this man at all. In fact, he was intriguing and he was known to the other people in the bar. There was nothing untoward about him or the atmosphere but how the hell did he know I was a sleepwalker?

He said he sensed something very spiritual in my presence and aura and this is why he was magnetized to me. I thought he was into something...well...you know what I mean. I was pleasantly surprised and relieved that all he wanted was to tell me about my sleepwalking and he gave me a valuable lesson in life that I was to cherish and use.

Aye, right! A life lesson? Did he mean never, ever, ever, use a car that is more than eight years old as the getaway vehicle? If that was his valuable lesson I could have taken that one, quite easily. I like the humour side of that. I was half-expecting something like that. I was sitting back and leaning forward with interest waiting on something like...

'You don't want to get caught out. Once four big burly gangsters have snatched their pension fund and retirement money – also known as a bank heist – and they are all dressed from head-to-toe in black, clutching two holdalls each, filled to the brim with enough money to buy twenty Concord planes and a small African country; brandishing sawn-off shot guns and yelling from behind their wee clown masks: *Go! Go! Go!* It's not a very good time to have to get out the car and go across the street and ask someone for a loan of their jump leads. Especially when it's raining.'

I was waiting on something like that because I was so used to punch lines and stuff not-so-serious. I was fae The Drum, if it wasn't a laugh it had to be serious. There wasn't much in between. I grew up with either a high or a low all around me. People laughed their heads off one minute and the next day they were gone. So meeting an Indian with advice for my life was going to have to be brilliant. It would have to top all the advice I have ever had and ever likely to have. Plenty of people in The Drum can give great advice. This guy better be good.

And he delivered.

He said my sleepwalking was a result of a wandering spirit I search of a place to unleash my creative greatness. I was a football player so I was thinking, he must mean scoring the best overhead kick or bending the best-ever free-kick the game has ever seen. I had no idea how right he would be some years later when I decided to take what he meant for real.

He also pointed out that the mainstream medical world often refer to sleepwalkers as having stress. I didn't have any stress. I was brought up in a great way and in a great environment. This Indian guy might be right, after all, I was thinking. I had not one shred of stress or pressure in my life whatsoever. Now this guy, who really shouldn't know anything about me, is telling me my sleepwalking is because of my soul and wandering spirit. This is a bit much to take in. I'm fae The Drum.

The Indian gentleman also told me that all we ever need in this world to succeed, survive, grow, expand and be happy is already in front of our noses. All the experience we have gone through in life are lessons to use. We do not need to look anywhere else in order for this formula to work.

That last part is more true than what we can otherwise imagine. Some of us fail in life because we don't use this formula and there is nothing magical about it, as the Indian pointed out. We all have it and we all have the capacity and ability to use it.

Knowing that my sleepwalking was not related to anything medical, it didn't as such become a relief as I never suffered from anything of the sort anyway, but the fact this guy just knew what he was talking about. I still can't get my head around how he knew I was a sleepwalker but all I know is, he knew and he was right. That is all I need to know.

I have always had difficulty in explaining my sleepwalking antics but even more so: my Indian connection.

I was telling a friend of mine about Indians and how they are very spiritual people.

He asked me what Indians I meant and I said, 'American Indians.'

They don't like the term Native Indians.

He said, 'Oh, I thought you meant the other ones.'

'What other ones?'

'Erm, well, you know, the other ones, *the other Indians.*'

I saw the look in his eyes trying to come up with what he meant as the *other Indians*. I just kept him going then he snapped his fingers and said, 'The cricket ones who eat curry, buy all their stuff at a Cash 'n Carry, and sell T-shirts.'

And you wonder why I have always had trouble explaining my spiritual encounters.

My sleepwalking goes back to a very young age. The most remarkable thing is the knowing you are sleepwalking comes to you days after. I have never been aware of my sleepwalking when it happened. I didn't walk the streets at night in my pyjamas and bare feet thinking, 'I'm sleepwalking here, I better put my slippers and a jacket on.' It just comes to you but the days that followed it would come to my mind and I could describe all the details.

It was a frosty night at around 2am. I got up, opened the door and left for an adventure. I was gone without making a noise. I had to walk down the hall and I didn't even need to avoid the squeaky floorboards because I was probably not aware they existed or I didn't care. That is one part of sleepwalking you don't have: a choice. You just sort of float through the whole experience.

I left the close and turned left. My intention was unclear but I walked around Fettercairn Avenue and I was attracted to the glittering frost underfoot. I was neither fazed nor worried. I obviously never met anyone because I would have been marched back to the house. All our neighbours were close to each other and all the kids were known. I have no doubt whatsoever that I would have been returned safely.

I turned back and headed up to Ian Mill's close. I remember going all the way up the stairs and reading all the names on the name plates. I never chapped any doors but I stood at Ian's door for what seemed like an eternity. I didn't chap the door and I had no motive to go there at that time in the morning. I just wandered. Had anyone opened the door they would have had the fright of their lives.

I would go up and down all the closes with not a care in the world. It is really weird because the slightest movement or scent would have triggered a dog to bark and we had a few dogs in our area. The Mills had their dog and the Johnstones' dogs would have sniffed me out anytime. Tania and Blitz were two Dobermans that let nothing go by them. I escaped their radar on many of my sleepwalking excursions.

I would often unlock the door and head off into the night. I did this on so many occasions it is virtually uncountable. No matter the safety precautions my parents took, there was no stopping this wee wandering spirit.

I almost made it to Clydebank but thanks to a late night stair scrub from our neighbour, Mrs Richardson, my proposed barefoot trip was rumbled.

I left the house as I always did. Pyjamas and barefeet. I walked all over the freshly-scrubbed Dettol and even stepped over the bucket and squeezed my way passed Mrs Richardson who said hello before continuing with her stair scrub. I was out of the close and turned right. Now, in Inchfad we were only a walk across a field to Clydebank. The carriageway was the biggest hurdle and not a good idea at any time to cross. Previously I had made it across the field, walking over jaggy nettles and rough terrain. I don't know what stopped me from achieving the ultimate but I always stopped halfway and three-quarters of the way and turned back. It was nothing to do with the dark because I was already a large part of the way over there.

I got to the end of the street, near where Campbell Johnstone lived when Mrs Richardson followed me and stopped me from going any further. She lived above me and maybe, just maybe, she saved me from a possible disaster. We will never know.

Later, when I became an adult she told me she had never been so relieved but she never got over the fact that it took her so long to react. In our close the neighbours had a rota system and each took their turn in cleaning the stairs. It was flexible and not regimented. Our close was spotless and the neighbours took pride in keeping the close clean. Mrs Richardson was standing in for Mrs Russell, taking her turn. It was close to midnight, but such was the rota system and the great teamwork, those stairs were getting cleaned. This is why Mrs Richardson was up late attending to the cleaning chores. She thought I was heading down to Mrs Russell's house at the ground floor to see Fergie and at one point she thought I was staying with the Russells and I went upstairs to my own house to use the bathroom. Those thoughts crossed Mrs Richardson's mind before she took off and saved me just steps away from me heading headlong into the open dark fields.

My sleepwalking habit should have prevented me from taking part in sleepovers and going away. I think most parents would be embarrassed and terrified but I was always given every opportunity to live as best I could. It was not a medical condition; contrary to what the medical profession say, it was just a creative and expanding mind in search of his wandering spirit.

Fergie Russell's big brother, William and his mum were discussing a holiday and my name was mentioned alongside Thomas Grant's. William and his girlfriend Roberta, who are now man and wife, had plans for a trip away with their crowd of friends and it sounded to me like I was going with them. I think they knew I was listening but played that silly adult game like I was not supposed to know. It was already agreed and arranged by all parties and my parents naturally approved. I didn't think they would take me due to my sleepwalking. At that time my sleepwalking was getting more and more frequent.

I asked Mr Russell if I was going on holiday with them. At this point I thought Mr & Mrs Russell were going, too.

'Am I allowed to go wi yous, Mr Russell?'

'Go where?'

'On holiday. Yous are going on holiday and you want tae take me wi ye.'

'No me.'

'But, I heard yous saying my name.'

'Aye, were aw gaun tae *Hame'lldaeme.*'

Mr Russell was a joker. He was forever playing jokes and his sense of humour was something to be cherished.

'Okay, we're aw gaun tae Jersey,' he announced.

'Jersey?'

'Aye, it's a great wee place. D'ye want tae see it?'

'Aye, okay. Show me.'

Mr Russell put his hands up his jumper (jersey) and stuck his tongue out.

A few minutes later Mrs Russell and William came

out from the kitchen and Mrs Russell asked me if I would like to go on my holidays with William, Roberta and Fergie. I needed no persuasion. I knew my parents had approved so there was no more need for discussions. It was all arranged and we were all going off on a holiday that would change my life.

When you are so young you don't carry worry but I do remember thinking that if I sleepwalk when I am away I will probably end up walking back to Drumchapel to my own bed. I consulted Mr Russell about this. It wasn't a fear but in the off-chance I would take off from my holidays I would try to return home. Mr Russell assured me that where I was going I would be getting a phone call from the Guinness Book of Records as the first and only wee boy to have walked the length of Scotland in his bare feet and pyjamas.

'Scotland?'

'Aye, yer gaun up North fir yer holidays.'

'I thought I was going tae Jersey?'

'Aye, that jersey.' (Putting his two hands up his pullover again).

Well, that holiday I shall explain in brief as this book is about the Drum but in my twenties I left Scotland and lived on the Isle of Jersey for a whole two years and two months, to be exact. When I returned for my annual Christmas holidays to Scotland I would head back to The Drum to visit my old haunt. On my very first visit back to Drumchapel since being on the island of Jersey, it was Mr Russell who opened the door to me. Before I entered the house, he asked me where I'd been. I stuffed my two fists up my pullover and stuck my tongue out.

He laughed, led me inside and cuffed me around the ear. It was, and always has been, the best and most recognizable welcome home ritual for a wee boy fae The Drum. I cannot get enough of it.

Our holiday up North was sensational. We toured for a fortnight. I never ventured out on my own at all hours. I had two weeks off sleepwalking. We even stayed at the famous Carbisdale Castle. The castle was rumoured to be haunted. Well, if there was ever a time to go sleepwalking it would have been then. Had I gone sleepwalking I might have made a name for myself and become a bigger and more realistic attraction than the Loch Ness Monster. But sadly, YouTube had not been invented then. They say timing is everything.

My sleepwalking increased. One night when I was sleepwalking, my dad decided to join me. We both had a sleepwalking experience at the same time. As the neighbours were running around trying to catch me, my dad was trying all the car doors. What is remarkable is not that both a father and son were out sleepwalking at the same time. It was the fact that my dad was trying all the car doors: and he was a policeman.

I stopped sleepwalking in my teens, had occasional experiences in my early twenties, but nothing after that until I moved to Germany where I had one last swing before I finally hung my pyjamas up.

The Indian was right all along. I stopped sleepwalking when I finally found my wandering spirit.

Luckily YouTube was not invented yet as I am not

sure I would have done the tourist industry any favours. You see, that holiday up North was still my best holiday but the Loch Ness Monster thing kinda gets on my...you know what.

They named her wrong. It's too obvious to be called Nessie. It would have been a lot more believable if she was named something more frightening like THE FINAL **NESS**DINATION or something. You know, to scare the fuck out of people a bit more. Nessie is just too nice. She needs a complete makeover. First those long eyelashes have to go. That makes her look like a loveable character. We need a monster who is gonna rip people's heads off and take all their social security benefits off of them.

Go home! There's nothing to see. Want proof? Okay, here's the deal...they have supersonic equipment that can be submerged under sea on a far away place like the east coast of America; like New York City. With that equipment they can see a guy fishing off a pier in the west coast of Ireland – and yet they cannot find a giant orphaned and abandoned eel in a fucking puddle? Give me a break.

I hate that fucking Loch Ness Monster crap. It's hilarious to even think this crap qualifies for a myth. Myths are mystical and interesting. Nessie is a fucking adult money-making fairytale gone wrong.

Go home, there's nothing to see.

Tourist industry: stop selling silly little ceramic ornaments in their three-piece glory with a stupid fucking jimmy hat on the poor bugger's heid. Do you honestly think if there was such a thing as a Loch Ness Monster he or she would pop up from under the dark mirky waters wearing a fucking tartan jaggy bunnet? No, it wouldn't, so go home, there's nothing to see.

Japanese people: take your cameras and go film capture something more tangible like a fucking visible building because there is nothing in Loch Ness to see.

American people: stop buying fucking radar equipment; it is a waste of money. Go home, there is nothing to see. It's all a con and a great big money swindle.

Do you know why they can't find Nessie? Because she doesn't fucking exist. It really is that simple so go home because there is nothing to see. Take your cameras, your tents, your wee bobbling-on-the-waves satellite boats and go back to where you belong because you are wasting your fucking time. I am doing you all a favour here by telling you something you should already know…and that is the truth. Be grateful.

In a way Jesus is like the Loch Ness Monster. If both ever turned up at a police station and handed in their particulars; got a DNA swob and was proven to be both the Holy Messiah and the monster it would shatter people's belief system. They would not take the news well because it would then eliminate the whole mystery of their existence.

The Drum:
The Final Goodbye
(excerpt from the Overspill Diaries)

It was a balmy day on August 19th, 1976. Ironically it was Mrs Russell's birthday. Mrs Russell was our downstairs neighbour and with her, her husband Willie, and sons William and Fergus, were a huge part of my life and little did I know would go on to become and even bigger part as the years went on.

My parents kept me and my sister away from all the flitting nonsense. We were to play with our mates as normal as if nothing in our world was about to change. It was quite philosophical, I must say, and I suppose it was the best thing for them and us.

The flitting wasn't done in one overnight swoop. Why should it? We weren't running from anything.

Our family were very young and it was time for a change. Like all good parents they just wanted the best for us. My sister and I shared one room and we were getting a wee bit older. One day the time would come that we had to have our own space and my parents knew that, so well, they were brave enough to make that decision.

It was a decision that would change my life forever. I only had friends in Drumchapel. I never really ventured outside it. It was my whole world. I had my best friends and a good part of my family all grew up and still lived there. I shudder at times to think what a move it was. It wasn't and couldn't have been an easy decision for anyone.

We were allocated a house just outside Hamilton. It

was a brand new S.S.H.A. (Scottish Special Housing Association) house in a brand new estate named Little Earnock.

The idea was to get there first then look for an exchange to my mother's intended target, East Kilbride. At the current rate there was no way we would have been offered a house in the new town as the waiting list was way too long and quite congested.

I'd heard of our new house but I was a bit young to understand much. I cannot say I was that excited about moving away but I was attracted to the fact I was to have my own room. Well, I was a kid and kids do think in selfish mode, at times.

As the days and weeks rolled on to the 19th of August our house was looking more empty. All our small stuff was gone and we were left with the bulk.

It was quite exciting as my Uncle Kenny was due any minute now with his big truck. Well, it wasn't his but as far as I was concerned he owned it! I can still hear the hissing of the front end as he parked it outside the house. It was huge. A big giant rental truck blocked all our usual view to St Laurence's football pitch, to Glasgow airport's runway view, where as small children we'd often sit in the long grass and make pretend bets, licking our thumbs for a seal of contract, on which way the plane would go after its take off.

August 19th was not only the day my life would change forever and it being Mrs Russell's birthday; it was also my Uncle Kenny's birthday, too. They say things come in threes. Well, that was a spooky hat-trick, right there. Uncle Kenny let me sit in the cab of the truck. You do feel quite special being above life but it was quite scary. I kept thinking what it must be like to go downhill in such a high up cab with a very flat in-your-face window.

To the other kids this giant truck parked outside our close must have looked like a UFO landing. It was not as if they hadn't seen one of these monsters before. The constant flow of traffic on the dual carriageway in our sights had one just about every 20th vehicle; but to actually be able to touch one was quite magnificent.

The neighbours started to pile out as all the little boys and girls scattered around the truck like wee monkeys at a safari park. They all scuttled away as more of our furniture was brought down to the front of the close.

The final piece of furniture was a lampshade. As my mum placed it securely in between a bunch of cushions: that was it. Out with the light and into the dark. Kenny closed the large doors at the back and the metal squeaked through the dry oil. *Clunk*! That was it. The final seal of my days in Drumchapel was now real. This is when it hit home that all my toddler and young childhood days were gone in one close of a truck's door.

The only time I've ever witnessed a goodbye ceremony in a close was when someone was going on holiday or if a wedding party were being picked up in their cars. I experienced both in such a short space of time. Not long before my Drumchapel departure we all said our goodbyes to the Grant family as they headed out for a holiday in Germany and when my Uncle Kenny was getting married we had a *scramble* in the car outside our close.

I confess to this day I did take part in a money scam

when I prearranged with Fergie Russell so he would benefit more than the other kids. I threw out a few coins to the right and all the kids all fought for the coins except for Fergie. He was waiting patiently for me to throw *his* share to the left.

Those were the only close encounters we had in the ceremonial theme until the 19th August 1976. There were adult tears. I could see everyone all hugging each other. Mrs Russell took it really bad. She was the very first neighbour we got to know when we moved there and she was the last one to say her goodbyes.

We weren't a special family as all families were special and no doubt some other family would have received the same attention if they were leaving. It was a day I will never forget. I was in the truck sitting in the middle of Uncle Kenny – who was driving – and my dad.

As we pulled away in this giant monster I looked up at my room window then the living-room and the close became smaller and smaller in my sight as we drove down Inchfad Drive. I could see in the wing mirrors some kids chasing the truck and some waved goodbye. Had I been older I might have been more emotional but I was too young. I was wrapped up in this big adventure. Unlucky for me I was not in the cab all the way to Hamilton but to Heathcot Ave to stay one last night in The Drum with my nana. She would look after us as the flitting was going on miles away. My parents didn't want my sister and I to be involved in the flitting and knowing what she's like she'd have wanted us to have a fully-fitted house to move into and have our rooms all ready.

That whole day at my nana's was torture. I was

desperate to go out and play with my mates but I was not allowed outside of her sight. Later at tea-time she finally gave in. I was allowed to go out in the back or as far as the top end of Heathcot but under no terms was I allowed to cross the busy Drumry Road on my own. It must have been a big responsibility for my nana and I am not sure how I would have reacted had I been in her position.

I was a very well-behaved boy but on this occasion the temptation got the better of me. I was out in the back courts of Heathcot talking to Paul Grimes when I bolted through a gap in the wooden fence, through the close of a Drumry Road tenement and out into the busy street. I ran through another close on the opposite side of the road and up through another broken fence and up through another close in Abbotshall. It seemed like a lifetime as I knew I only had a small window to play with. My nana was very strict and she was not the one to mess with. I could see my old street up ahead as I raced across the pitches at Halgreen and up by the scout hall towards Inchfad. It was all uphill.

Tommy Rankin and Barry Grant were in the school playing with some other boys and when they saw me you'd have thought they'd seen a ghost.

'I thought you were away,' said wee Barry, as he clutched a stick in his hand.

'I am away but I am staying at my nana's until the morra then I go and live in ma new hoose.'

We played in the school when more kids got wind I was back in the street. Some thought it was a joke our family were playing because only hours earlier we had this big leaving ceremony in the close then I turn up again.

I could hear my name being called out by an adult and when an adult calls your name it was for two things: your dinner or you were in trouble. I wasn't expecting my dinner as I had mine earlier so I must have been in trouble. It was Mrs Russell summoning me to her house. Now, when Mrs Russell summoned you, you knew you were in for it.

She ripped right into me. She knew the plan that I was to stay at my nana's for that day and night so my parents and some help from Stewart, my other uncle, could get the new house furnished up. Mrs Russell was raging; not that I was back as she was pleased to see me; but she knew I had betrayed my nana's trust in me.

Mrs Russell and my nana were the only ones I knew of who each had a phone in their houses. I am sure others had but only those two had one each that I remember and I can still recall their numbers.

I was ordered by Mrs Russell to go back and play with Barry and Tommy but I was to be back down at Heathcot for 7pm. This meant Mrs Russell had called my nana to confirm my whereabouts.

On my return to Heathcot at 7pm my nana said nothing. She never acknowledged that she knew I had skipped it back up to Inchfad. She never let on.

The next day I was gone. I would not return to The Drum for some time later. There was a settling in process to be had and as painful as it was, we had to go through it.

Turning left at the roundabout on Drumry Road, we headed down the dual carriageway on Great Western Road. Looking out the back window again I could see Drumchapel getting smaller and smaller until it finally disappeared.

I'd been told what this new place was like. My Uncle Stewart told me the most about the place. It was full of kids and what's more: it was full of Glasgow kids.

Little Earnock was situated on the edge of Hamilton towards the East Kilbride end. Many say the plan was to join both together at some point but they haven't managed that as yet and I am not sure if the actually have plans but East Kilbride was only a short trip up the back roads from Little Earnock.

The smell of the house was all new stuff. Wall panels, the floor and my room was amazing. It faced the very quiet back and my sister's was larger, had a low-level window and faced the front. It was eery on the first night trying to get to sleep. The stillness of the night kept me awake. I had never known such quiet. I kept hearing the voices of Mrs Russell giving me into trouble, my nana's instructions and wee Barry and Tommy's laughter as I frightened them on my ghostly return.

Little Earnock was a million miles away from anything I ever dreamed of. We finally reached that Peter & Jane level of having a back-and-front door, up-and-down-stairs and our own garden to hang out the washing. We had a wee yellow whirly washing line that rotated. It was like a swing in our back garden. Pure Peter & Jane book stuff.

There were no problems in meeting friends. Everyone I knew in the first couple of days were all Glaswegians. Graham and Greig Bell came from the Paisley Road West area; Ronnie and George Darroch plus their wee sisters came from Castlemilk; and would you believe it? I met a boy from The Drum.

Steven Marshall was a Drummy boy and he made me feel I was not so far away after all.

Later my family moved and finally settled in East Kilbride and there I found another overspill family in the Youngs. I had to do it all over again with another new town, another new school and another new crowd of friends. Mr & Mrs Young helped me brilliantly to settle. They came from Priesthill and I became friends and an unofficial adopted son and integrated into their family.

I heard some of the old neighbours say some really weird things. I didn't know at the time but they were just clichés, sayings and phrases made only for adults' understanding.

'Whit's the matter wi ye, son, has the cat got yer tongue?'

I just left all my friends and the closest neighbourhood anyone is ever likely to grow up in and an adult asks me about a stupid cat?

Any time I heard a football commentator say, 'They're not out of the woods yet,' I would think they must be talking about the Bluebell Woods. And I often wondered if the number 20 or even the number 9 could actually take me to Square One if ever I was in trouble. 'It must be near George Square,' I'd say to myself.

As a show of appreciation to all the adults in my street who ever used a phrase or a cliché on me, I bring you the following:

Before I die I want to sit on a **purple patch** and finally get my hands on the sharp instrument that people use to **cut a long story short.**

I will do it with all my mite although I don't have much money I shall carry out my operation **on a shoestring budget.**

Then I will keep going until I reach my goal and I will not give up until **the fat lady sings.**

After I have accomplished this I will then go and study **rocket science** – as it seems quite needed these days. If someone wants to join me I will just say what one blind boxer said to the other blind boxer: **'Knock yourself out.'**

I don't go about life **sweating the small stuff** because to me, it is not really important to see what and how people do when they **step up to the plate** that everyone keeps talking about. I would rather watch people **hit the ground running.** To me, that sounds a lot more entertaining.

Well, **life's too short.** It has to be because there is nothing in this world longer. No street, no journey from one continent to another, and certainly no piece of string.

I cherish life. I was approached by this hooded mugger in the city centre and he said: **'I'll beat you within one inch of your life,'** so I stepped back a few feet. I like to give these people some work to do because I have a life to live but not the life others want. Others want a house and **2.5 children** but I don't know how I would cope with a midget in the family.

Many people told me I was **making a rod for my own back** by choosing to live in The Drum but comments like that don't bother me. If one thing I learned growing up in the best place in the world it was: things that hit you right **out of the blue** don't necessarily mean you are **not out of the woods yet**

289

and I have never been afraid to speak my mind. My Drumchapel upbringing has made me who I am and what I say. The **cat will never get my tongue.**

I learned so many things from my Drumchapel background. I got to know what **revenge tastes like** and it's kind of sweet, right enough.

So, people, just enjoy your life because **you could get knocked down by a bus**…unless you crossed the road in one of those **month of Sundays** then you will be alright because you picked the best day to stay alive.

But **don't put all your eggs in one basket** otherwise you will **miss the boat;** although to be honest you can miss a train, a plane or a bus but unless you happen to be the ones who didn't get on the Titanic or the guy in the Milk Tray advert I think you'll be just quite fine.

Be cautious in life. Your Drumchapel upbringing will have taught you many things and if you apply yourself correctly you can achieve absolutely anything you want in life but just remember and stay humble. No matter how good you are or how brilliant you become you will never be able to **make something out of thin air.** There are the chosen ones who can pull this off like a scientist, a doctor in physics, or the girl from Blue Peter. She can go to the high altitude in the Bolivian mountains, bring back an empty jar, open the lid in the studio in front of millions of viewers, empty the thin air out and make a paper mâché hat.

On a last note, just remember when someone promises you something and they do not fullfil that promise, just say what one wee fish out of water said to the other wee fish out of water: **'Don't hold your**

breath any.'

And when someone asks you to **draw a line under the sand** ask them to first take you to the seaside then force them to hand you a stick and let them point exactly where they want that line drawn; but be quick, before the tide comes in otherwise your lasting statement will not be contractually valid. If you don't complete this task, don't bother going **back to the drawing board** because none exists. It is a phrase made up for an excuse for failing at everything in life.

If you can't do any of the above then sorry, you will have to go **back to square one.**

Live life the easy way, if you can…dare I say…**like blowing feathers off of the Linkwood flats.**

The Drum:
The Legends

Annette Ballantyne

Legend of The Drum

Annie Will

Legend of The Drum

Carol Ann Davis

Legend of The Drum

Carol Wallace

Legend of The Drum

Caroline Agnew

Legend of The Drum

Catherine McKnight

Legend of The Drum

Elizabeth Brennan

Legend of The Drum

George Hall

Legend of The Drum

Isobel Murphy

Legend of The Drum

Isobel Stewart

Legend of The Drum

James Campbell

Legend of The Drum

Jeannette Gilchrist

Legend of The Drum

Jessie Reilly

Legend of The Drum

Joyce Miller

Legend of The Drum

Laura Cullen

Legend of The Drum

Linda Donaghy

Legend of The Drum

Margaret Riddick

Legend of The Drum

Margaret Will

Legend of The Drum

Mary Donnelly

Legend of The Drum

Mary McGreskin

Legend of The Drum

Mr & Mrs Gilchrist

Legends of The Drum

Mr & Mrs Best

Legends of The Drum

Mr & Mrs Grant

Legends of The Drum

Mr & Mrs
John & Agnes Nicol

Legends of The Drum

Mr & Mrs Johnstone

Legends of The Drum

Mr & Mrs McLafferty

Legends of The Drum

Mr & Mrs Rankin

Legends of The Drum

Mr & Mrs Reilly

Legends of The Drum

Mr & Mrs Richardson

Legends of The Drum

Mr & Mrs Russell

Legends of The Drum

Mr & Mrs Savage

Legends of The Drum

Mr & Mrs Scott

Legends of The Drum

Mr & Mrs Trainer

Legends of The Drum

Mr & Mrs Vernon

Legends of The Drum

Mr & Mrs Wylie

Legends of The Drum

Mr Kidd

Legend of The Drum

Mr McGroarty

Legend of The Drum

Mr Pennie

Legend of The Drum

Mrs Degnan

Legend of The Drum

Mrs Gracie

Legend of The Drum

Mrs Stewart

Legend of The Drum

Norah McGrail

Legend of The Drum

Rena Dougall

Legend of The Drum

Robert Henderson

Legend of The Drum

Ronnie McCabe

Legend of The Drum

Stuart Ainslie

Legend of The Drum

Thomas Reid

Legend of The Drum

Timothy Gattens

Legend of The Drum

Tommy Blair

Legend of The Drum

Walter Matuszczyk

Legend of The Drum

William McGready

Legend of The Drum

William Roberts

Legend of The Drum

The Final Dedication

Hopefully this book has helped you to look back on the great times we had growing up in The Drum. We also hope you have felt some comfort in the memories and reading your loved ones' names. It is important to be reminded of those who are no longer with us in the physical world, because they gave us all something to look back on and to help us look forward.

Many are so glad we grew up in the decades in which we did. Life would not be fair if all we had to look back on was a high-tech pay-as-you-go world. The internet has been great for getting back in touch with those who shared our roots but we would not be so willing to search our Drum mates had it not been for the great times we had with them when we had less.

Give us a lollipop stick and a game of kick-the-can, any day of the week.

The Matuszczyk Family: Walter, Jessie, Anthony, Christopher, John, Mark, Robert, Big Tim (Jessie's brother), Janet, Ian, Lawson (The Campbells), Willie Robertson, his mum & dad and his wee sisters; Mr & Mrs Henderson from Drumry Road, son Robert and family; John Ayre, Paul Gracie, Stephen and Eddie Brennan, Stuart Ainslie, Donaghy family, Kurt McInnes, William and Allan Wright, Barry Devlin, John McGhee, Mr & Mrs Lowe, Mark McGhee, Ian Mills, Irene Mills, Frank, Maureen and Celia Deans; The Mills family and Glen (the dog); Smyth family, May Donnelly, Smart family, Steele family, Mr & Mrs

Semple, Mary Donnelly, Jackie Varney, McPhillie family, Terry Carberry, Mrs Stewart, Burns family, Ingalls family, Mr & Mrs McSkimming, Delaney family, Karen Green, Margaret Rose Aitken, Alison Brown, Nan Stewart, Julie Ainslie, Donald McCreadie, Brown Family, Carberry family, Team family, O'Neil family, Workman family, Deans family, Ants and Steven Clarke, Clarke family, Donnelly family, McGonigle family, Black family, McSeveny family, Betty Oliver, John Macpherson, Mrs Morrison, Alison Craig, Mr & Mrs Williams, Mr & Mrs Low, Pat and Vince Burgoyne, Burgoyne family, McCreadie family, Ingles family, Robertson family, Johnson family, McClure family, Miller family, Mrs Gracie, Grimes family, Holt family, Ronnie Carroll, Tam Carroll, Joe Donachie, Betty Barclay, Louise Barclay, Kenny Barclay, Billy Barclay, Gerard Barclay; Revel family, Annette Ballantyne, Shug Monroe, McMillan family, Watson family, McCourt family, Jimmy Stewart, Kenny Campbell, Mrs Sloan, Jim Bryson, Gordon Hamilton, Jim Campbell, Crawford family, Ripley family, Steven MacDonald, Dollan family, White family, Dougan family, Watters family, Mr & Mrs Chalmers, Big Harry, McKellar family, Mr & Mrs Jamieson, Kelt family, Faulkner family, Hope family, Thompson family, John Rippey, Nicky Burrows and Lynne McIntyre.

To all the kids who grew up in all the streets of Drumchapel. A very special thanks for their inclusion and their stories: Big Auntie Madge, Archie *fae up the sterrs,* Dougie, Tam, and their wives, *Auld* Betty, and *The Weans.*

Many thanks to all who contributed to
The Drum: The People's Story

A Publication by SHN Publishing
www.shnpublishing.com

Lightning Source UK Ltd.
Milton Keynes UK
UKOW04f0953170216

268540UK00001B/36/P